October 1985

KU-714-810

# BLOOD BROTHERS

**Elias Chacour** is ordained in the Melkite
Church, an ancient body of believers that has
existed in the Middle East from the earliest
centuries of Christianity. Educated in Paris at
the *Seminaire du Saint Sulpice*, Chacour was
the first Palestinian to earn a degree from the
Hebrew University where he studied Bible and
Talmud. Currently he is building schools,
libraries, community centres and youth clubs
throughout Israel's Galilee region.

# BLOOD BROTHERS

**ELIAS CHACOUR**

with David Hazard

KINGSWAY PUBLICATIONS
EASTBOURNE

Copyright © Elias Chacour 1984

First published in the USA by Chosen Books,
Lincoln, Virginia,
a division of the Zondervan Corporation

First British edition 1985

All rights reserved.
No part of this publication may be reproduced or
transmitted in any form or by any means, electronic
or mechanical, including photocopy, recording, or any
information storage and retrieval system, without
permission in writing from the publisher.

ISBN 0 86065 328 5

*Front cover design by Vic Mitchell*

Printed in Great Britain for
KINGSWAY PUBLICATIONS LTD
Lottbridge Drove, Eastbourne, E. Sussex BN23 6NT by
Cox & Wyman Ltd, Reading.

# *Contents*

# Dedication

To my father who will not be mentioned in the world history books, though he is written in the heart of God as His beloved child: Michael Moussa Chacour from Biram in Galilee, refugee in his own country and one who speaks the language of patience, forgiveness and love.

And to my brothers and sisters, the Jews who died in Dachau; and my brothers and sisters, the Palestinians who died in Tel-azzaatar, Sabra and Shatila refugee camps.

# An Urgent Word Before

Before I had set my hands to the typewriter keys I was aware that this could be "a controversial book." The reason is that *Blood Brothers* breaks new ground in what has been written about the Middle East turmoil and goes beyond the usual political wrestlings over "who owns the land?" It will disturb certain people and please others, and for the same reason: it probes those ever-murky areas of conscience and heart. Above all, this is a story about people, not politics.

Before I had heard of Elias Chacour (pronounced shah-*koor*), I was not aware that I held certain prejudices regarding Middle East issues. Leafing through the *Sojourners Magazine* one afternoon, I was stopped by an article entitled, "Children of Ishmael in the Promised Land,"* by Jim Forest, and pored through an arresting interview with Chacour, a Palestinian Christian leader. I was amazed at my mixed response.

What moved me was his soul-felt cry for reconciliation between Palestinians and Jews and his obvious love for both. I was stirred by reading about a side of the Arab-Israeli

---

* *Sojourner's Magazine*, September 1980.

conflict that is little known. Yet something was interfering with my sympathies.

Had I not heard countless news reports about Arab terrorism and the Palestinian Liberation Organization? I had never considered that there were also Palestinian Christians who were living the challenging, non-violent alternative taught by Jesus Christ in the midst of the world's most bitter conflict. Why had I never heard of Chacour and his people before?

Forest's interview stuck with me a long time, like a nail in my conscience. Finally, in the spring of 1983, it spurred a trip to Galilee where I was to meet Chacour in his small village of Ibillin. Perched on the green hills northeast of Nazareth, overlooking the citrus groves along the Mediterranean, Ibillin has a mixed population of Christians and Moslems. There, my Western mentality towards Palestinians was exposed blatantly, and I felt chagrined.

Somehow I was expecting Chacour, the pastor of Ibillin's Melkite Church, to be naive and unsophisticated. Instead, I was captivated by this man of medium stature, barrel-chested, with a black, prophet-like beard that is streaked by a lightning slash of gray—an intense and intensely warm human being.

I discovered that Chacour is Paris-educated, holds a doctorate, speaks eleven languages including Ugaritic, the ancient mother tongue of both Hebrew and Arabic, and has a degree from the Hebrew University in Jerusalem. Moreover, his frequent travels carry him to several continents, to churches and synagogues, before queens and prime ministers. With each person he meets—Irish Catholic or Protestant, Indian or Pakistani, Gentile or Jew—he shares the secrets of lasting peace.

Neither was Ibillin what I expected in a Palestinian village.

True, the cinder-block houses, cramped against the road, are poor by Western standards; goats and donkeys wander about, and cats are anything but domesticated; in 1983 the village was just constructing its first high school building. But beneath the surface poverty, the life of the spirit is rich. Dramas and public poetry readings abound, teenagers dance and sing in honor of their mothers on a special day of celebration and the church is alive with young singing voices.

Nevertheless, I was challenged by Chacour's strong statements. Among them, that Palestinians have a God-given right to live in Israel as equals, though many Israelis claim the land is theirs exclusively and by scriptural mandate. And Chacour has a gentle impatience with those who come to Israel to venerate shrines of the past while ignoring human beings; who come to see only "holy stones and holy sand." With a spreading smile he directed his challenge at me: "Did you come for the shrines—or do you want to learn about the *living* stones?"

Preeminently, he was concerned that I was one more writer from the West who would present a cut-and-dried view of the Middle East. "Can you help me to say that the persecution and stereotyping of Jews is as much an insult to God as the persecution of Palestinians?" he begged. "I wish to disarm my Jewish brother so he can read in my eyes the words, 'I love you.' I have beautiful dreams for Palestinian and Jewish children together."

Our encounter sent me on a search for some truth amid the muddle of violence and recriminations, politics and spiritual claims. The fact that I was writing the story of one man's life did not make my work any easier. My strong desire to set Elias Chacour's personal story in perspective made writing painfully slow. And all the while my political opinions and my long-held beliefs about Bible prophecy were stretched further than I imagined possible.

What drove me to completing *Blood Brothers* was the human drama—the compassion and the rare treasure of peace within Elias Chacour that I wanted to discover for myself. His is a true account that moved me as few before—an account of faith in the midst of indignity, hatred and violence in the furnace that is the Middle East.

In that furnace, Elias' story begins.

David Hazard

# 1

# *News In the Wind*

Surely my older brother was confused. I could hardly believe what he was telling me. I leaned dangerously far out on a branch, my bare feet braced against the tree trunk, and accidentally knocked a scattering of figs down onto the head of poor Atallah who had just delivered the curious news.

"A celebration?" I shouted from my tilting perch. "Why are we having a celebration? Who told you?"

"I heard Mother say—" he called back, dodging the falling figs, "that something *very big* is happening in the village. And," he paused, his voice sinking to a conspiratorial hush, "Father is going to buy a lamb."

A lamb! Then it *must* be a special occasion. But why? It was still a few weeks until the Easter season, I puzzled, sitting upright on the branch. At Easter-time our family celebrated with a rare treat of roasted lamb—and for that matter it was one of the few times during the year that we ate meat at all. We knew—because Father always reminded us— that the lamb represented Jesus, the Lamb of God. And, of course, I realized that Father was not going to *buy* a lamb. We rarely bought anything. We bartered for items that we could not grow in the earth or make or raise ourselves, the same as everyone else in our village of Biram.

I'm sure Atallah knew that if he waited around, he was risking another barrage of figs and questions. He was already trotting away toward the garden plot beyond our small stone house where I should have been helping Mother and the rest to clear away rocks. It was an endless job even then, in 1947, since no one in our village of Biram owned farm machinery to make work easier. When school had ended an hour before, I had hidden up in this fig tree—my tree, as I called it—to escape the labor. Now, watching Atallah disappear, I wondered what exciting event was rippling the too-regular course of our lives.

*I must find Father and ask him myself,* I decided.

Instead of dropping down into the deep orchard grass to trail after Atallah, I shinnied higher up the fig tree—up to the very top, where the branches bent at dangerous angles under my weight. This was my special place. Besides being a good lookout post, it bore not one, but *six* different kinds of figs. My father, who was something of a wizard with fruit-bearing trees, had performed a natural magic called grafting and combined the boughs of five other fig trees onto the trunk of a sixth. A thick, curling vine trellised up the trunk and spread through the branches, too, draping the tree with clusters of mouth-puckering grapes. Many afternoons, I monkeyed my way up onto a high branch, sampling the juicy fruit until my stomach cramped. Then I would ease down into Mother's cradling arms and she would comfort me, her littlest boy— her dark-haired, spoiled one.

"Elias," she would coo over me, shaking her head. "You'll never learn, will you? And I would bury my face in her thick hair, groaning as my four older brothers and my sister rolled their eyes in disgust.

Now, with one arm crooked around the topmost branch, I

pushed aside the curled leaves, thrusting my head out into the spring sun which was slanting toward late afternoon. Perhaps Father was in his orchard. Row after row of fig trees spread for several acres, stretching down the hill away from our house, covering the slope with rustling greenery. The broadening leaves concealed a fresh-water spring and a dark, mossy grotto where our goats and cattle sheltered themselves in summer. Beyond our orchards rose the lush majestic highlands of the upper Galilee. They looked purple in the distance—"the most beautiful land in all of Palestine," Father said so often. A dreamy look would mist into his pale blue eyes then, as it did whenever he spoke about his beloved land.

Search as I might, I could not find Father ambling among those trees just now. Most days he worked there with my brothers, teaching them the secrets of husbandry. At seven years old, I was considered too young—and too impish—to learn about the fig trees. With or without me, my father and brothers had busheled up three tons of golden-brown figs in the last harvest.

With a recklessness that would have paled my mother, I swung down from the treetop and flung myself to the ground. Then I was off, running toward the center of the village. Surely someone had seen Father.

I darted through the narrow streets—hardly streets at all, but foot-worn, dirt corridors that threaded the homes of the village together beneath the shade of cedar and silver-green olive trees—dodging a goat and some chickens in my path. Biram seemed like one huge house to me. Our family, the Chacours, had led their flocks to these, the highest hills of Galilee, many hundreds of years ago. My grandparents had always lived here, nearly next door to us. And there were so many aunts, uncles, cousins and distant relatives clustered here, it was as if each stone dwelling was merely another room where another bit of my family lived. All the homes fit snugly together right up to our own, the last house at the far edge of the village. Biram had grown here, quietly rearing its children, reaping its harvests, dozing beneath the Mediterranean stars for so many generations that all households were as one family.

And today this whole family seemed to be keeping a secret from me. I ran from house to house where small knots of kerchiefed women in long, dark skirts were talking with hushed excitement. Eagerly, I burst in on a group of older women, some of my many "grandmothers." They stopped clucking at each other only long enough to *shush* me and shoo me out the door again.

My feelings bruised, I trotted toward our church which was the living heart of Biram. Here the entire village crowded in on Sundays, shoulder to shoulder beneath its embracing stone arches. The parish house, a small stone building huddled next to the church, doubled as a schoolhouse during the week, its ancient foundations quaking from our noisy activities. This year was my first in school, and I loved it. Now, in the church's moss-carpeted courtyard, a group of men were talking loudly. Father was not among them, so I bounded off toward the open square just beyond.

Normally I hesitated before entering the square. This was the realm of men—especially the village elders—and it held a certain awe for me. Children were tolerated here only because we were plentiful as raindrops and just as unstoppable. However, we knew enough to keep a respectful margin between our foolish games and the clusters of men who came in the evening to hear news that the traveling merchants carried in from far-off villages along with their shiney pots, metal knives, shoes and what-not. Tottering at the edge of the square were the stoney, skeletal remains of an ancient synagogue. On this spot, Father had told us, the Roman Legions had built a pagan temple many centuries ago. The Jews later destroyed the temple and raised on its foundations a place of worship for the one, true God. Now the synagogue stood ruined and ghost-like, too. It was forbidden to play among the fallen pillars and any child brazen enough to do so suffered swift and severe punishment, for it was considered consecrated ground.

That day I shot out into the sun-bright square—and nearly toppled to a halt. The square, it startled me to see, was not abandoned to the clots of older men who usually nodded there in the afternoon warmth. Men young and old were huddled everywhere, talking about . . . *what?* Surely everyone had heard the news but me!

Impatiently, my dark eyes scanned the groups of men for Father's slender form. It was no use. Nearly all the men wore *kafiyehs*, the white, sheet-like headcoverings that shaded their heads from the Galilean sun and braced them from the wind. At a glance, almost any of them might be Father!

On tip-toe I carefully laced my way between these huddles, peering around elbows in search of that one lean, gentle face. The faces I saw looked pinched and serious. Whatever they were discussing was most urgent. Otherwise they would not be gathered here on a spring afternoon when fields wanted ploughing and trees awaited the clean slice of the pruning hook.

Not that I was eavesdropping, of course, but amid the murmur of discussion I picked up the fact that Biram was expecting a special visit. But *who* was coming? Visits by the Bishop were quite an event, but regular enough that they did not cause this kind of stir.

My sneaking was not altogether unnoticed, however. Poking my face into one circle of men, I stared up into a pair of black deepset eyes, belonging to one of the two *mukhtars* of Biram—a chief elder in the village. I tried to duck, but—

"What do you want here, Elias?" the *mukhtar's* voice was gravelly with an edge of sternness.

My face reddened. Would I ever learn not to barge into things?

"I . . . uh . . . have you seen my father? I have to find him—it's important." I hoped that I sounded convincing, and it was true enough since I was about to die with curiosity.

The sternness of his look eased a bit. "No Elias, I haven't seen him. He's probably—"

"I spoke with him earlier," another man interrupted. "He went trading today—I don't know where. Maybe over in the Jewish village." Then he stepped in front of me, closing the circle again. Thankfully, I was forgotten.

The Jewish village? Perhaps. As I fled from the square, I remembered that Father often went there to barter. Many of these Jewish neighbors came to Biram to trade as well. When they stopped by our house for figs, Father welcomed them with the customary hospitality and a cup of tar-like, bittersweet coffee—the cup of friendship. One man was a perfect marvel to me, roaring into our yard almost weekly in a sleek, black automobile—the first one I had ever seen.

At the far edge of town I stopped, craning my neck to look far down the road. It was empty. If Father was on his way to the Jewish village, he was long-gone.

My eagerness fizzled. And still I could not take my eyes off the road, hoping for some glimpse of him. Beyond the next hill, the road wound southward to Gish, our nearest neighboring village. And further down the valleys, not many kilometers, the Mount of Beatitudes rose up from the Sea of Galilee's northern shore. I could not see the Mount from where I stood and had never seen it for that matter, for even a few kilometers seemed a long journey from our mountain fastness.

Past the Sea of Galilee I knew almost nothing. I could not

imagine the unreal world beyond—a world that Father said had just warred against itself. I could not fathom such a thing. Mine was a peaceful world of fig and olive groves, countless cousins, aunts and uncles. Time passed almost seamlessly from one harvest to another, marked only births, deaths and holidays. I felt safe and sheltered here, as if the very arms of God embraced our hills like the strong, over-arching stones of our church.

Certainly, this was a child-like vision. Only vaguely was I aware of distant disturbances.

There had been trouble in the mid-1930s, before my birth. Father told us there had been opposition to the British who had driven out the Turks and now protected us under a temporary Mandate. Strikes and riots had shaken Jerusalem, Haifa and all of Palestine, but these were quickly quelled. It was just one more incident in the long history of armies that traversed or occupied our land. Then things had settled, so it appeared, into a lull. Soon, it was hoped, the British would establish a free Palestinian government, as they had promised. Without a single radio or newspaper in all Biram—even then, in the late 1940s—we had no inkling that a master plan was already afoot, or that powerful forces in Jerusalem, in continental Europe, in Britain and America were sealing the fate of our small village and all Palestinian people.

Standing dejectedly on the road from Biram, with the sun settling low and red on the hills, my only thoughts were of Father. And Mother . . . *oh no!* I had forgotten about Mother! Surely she would be home from the fields, upset to find that I'd wandered off again. My feet were flying before I'd finished the thought.

At the edge of our orchard, the sweet scent of woodsmoke from Mother's outdoor fire met me, and the steamy sweetness of baking bread. Mother was stooping over her metal oven which stood on a low grate next to the house. My sister, Wardi, fed sticks to the licking flames, and on the grate, a pot of tangy stuffed grape leaves boiled. My brothers were hauling wood and water. If only I could slip in quietly among them, Mother might not realize I'd been away . . . But Atallah spotted me first. Nearest to me in age, he was my best ally—and sometimes my dearest opponent.

A tell-all sort of smirk lit his face, and he announced in a clarion voice, "Mother, here's Elias now."

Mother looked up at me, the firelight playing about her pleasant, full face. A brightly colored kerchief drew her hair up in a bun. I cringed, expecting a sound scolding. At that moment, however, she seemed unusually distracted, her gentle eyes clouded in thought. "Go and help Musah carry the water," she murmured, waving me away.

Musah, who was the next oldest after Atallah, was beside me in an instant. He thrust an empty bucket at me. "Get busy," he ordered with a triumphant grin.

I had to know before I exploded. "Mother, what's happening in Biram? Is Father buying a lamb? Is it a celebration?"

"Take the bucket," Musah demanded, his grin fading.

"Mother, tell me. Everyone knows but me and—"

"A celebration? Well, yes. Perhaps. Father wants to tell you himself. I said go help your brother."

"Take the bucket," said Musah, thumping me with it.

"*Mother,*" I stomped impatiently. At that moment, a familiar voice called to me through the trees.

"Hello, Elias. I'm glad to see such a happy helper." From the shadowy green darkness beneath the fig boughs, a lean figure stepped out into the circle of firelight. Behind him, led by a short cord of rope, was a yearling lamb.

Father was home!

When Father returned home at the end of each day he

brought with him a certain, almost mystical calm. His eyes lit up in the flicker of firelight and a placid smile always turned up the corners of his thick mustache. At his appearance, disputes between children ceased instantly. For one thing, Father was stern with his discipline. Play was one matter, but rude behavior did not befit the children of Michael Chacour. More than that, I believe we all felt the calm that seemed to lift Father above the squabbles of home or village. Above all, Father was a man of peace.

I raced to catch his hand, absolutely dying to ask a million questions. The weary slump of his shoulders made me think better of it. Father was no longer a young man, in fact, he was almost fifty. His light brown hair and mustache were tinged with silver-gray. For once I held my tongue, and instead, quietly stroked the lamb's dusty-white face.

Turning to Mother he smiled. "Katoub, has the Lord sent us anything to feed these hungry children?"

Mother knew, without Father's gentle hints, that he too was hungry and footsore. "Come children—quickly," she said, sparking into action. She waved Musah off to the stable on the far side of the house to pen the lamb. Then she mustered the rest of us into a circle around the fire. It was our daily drill: children were organized and quieted, for evenings belonged to Father.

If some important news was in the wind, Father did not seem ruffled by it in the least. No matter that I was about to split in half with curiosity! He accepted a steaming plate of food from Mother, settling with a regal quietness beside the sputtering fire.

Just when I was certain I would explode, Father set aside his plate. "Come here, children. I have something special to tell you." he said, motioning for us to sit by him. It had grown fully dark and chilly, and I pressed in close at his side.

"In Europe," he began, and I noticed a sadness in his eyes,

"there was a man called Hitler. A Satan. For a long time he was killing Jewish people. Men and women, grandparents—even boys and girls like you. He killed them just because they were Jews. For no other reason."

I was not prepared for such horrifying words. *Someone killing Jews?* The thought chilled me, made my stomach uneasy.

"Now this Hitler is dead," Father continued. "But our Jewish brothers have been badly hurt and frightened. They can't go back to their homes in Europe, and they have not been welcomed by the rest of the world. So they are coming here to look for a home.

"In a few days, children," he said, watching our faces, "Jewish soldiers will be traveling through Biram. They are called *Zionists*. A few will stay in each home, and some will stay right here with us for a few days—maybe a week. Then they will move on. They have machine guns, but they don't kill. You have no reason to be afraid. We must be especially kind and make them feel at home."

I glanced at the others. What were they thinking? Wardi's face seemed a mixture of emotions. On the verge of womanhood, she was graceful and lithe as an olive branch, favoring Father's slenderness. I could not guess her thoughts. Next to her sat Rudah, my oldest brother. In the leaping firelight, he looked like an artist's study of Father in his younger days with fair skin, lighter hair, a narrow face and an aquiline nose. At his side was Chacour who, because of an old custom, had been given the improbable name of Chacour Chacour. Like Rudah, he sported the first faint shadow of a mustache. Though Chacour looked a little uneasy, Rudah's frown told me he was more deeply troubled. Musah and Atallah both sat stiffly quiet. In a few years, it seemed that they, too, would inherit Father's lean, wind-carved looks. Only I was dark, with black hair, olive skin and Mother's rounded face. And I did not know what to make of such news.

Father saw the somber look on all of our faces. With a sudden change of tone, he announced festively, "That's why I bought the lamb. We're going to prepare a feast. This year we'll celebrate the Resurrection early—for our Jewish brothers who were threatened with death, and are alive."

Then Atallah was right. We were celebrating. The strange chill mood was broken.

"And the best news of all," Father continued, a child-like spark of fun in his eyes, "the best news is that you will get to sleep up on the roof."

Sleep on the roof! Wonderful! Our house roof was flat, as were most of the roofs in Biram. On summer nights when it was too hot in the loft where we children slept, we were allowed to sleep up there under the stars. On these cold spring nights we would have to bundle up, but the skies would be brilliantly clear and star-strewn.

Before the excitement bubbled over entirely, Father quieted our cheering. As usual, we would finish our mealtime with family prayers. I crept onto Mother's lap, though I was really too big by then, and listened as Father bowed his head.

"Father in heaven," he began softly, "help us to show love to our Jewish brothers. Help us to show them peace to quiet their troubled hearts." As he continued, I imagined his words rising into the night sky like the smokey tendrils of incense that was burned at church. He finished with a soft "amen."

Mother was strangely quiet, and slipped inside where she lit a small fire on the hearth to warm the house. Later, the six of us children climbed the ladder to our sleeping loft, where a toastiness had gathered beneath the rafters. As we curled up beneath our blankets, we could hear Mother and Father beneath us, stirring the fire and talking in low voices.

In the coming days, Father would kill and prepare our lamb, and Mother would prepare vegetables and cakes, accepting, at least with surface calmness, the coming of the soldiers.

How could they have understood the new force that was invading our land? It was a force that our Jewish neighbors did not yet fully understand.

And as for me, a way was opening—a way of peace through bitter conflict. And I did not know.

For now, I edged up against Atallah. My breathing slipped into a slow rhythm with his. And I slept for one of the very last nights in my own house.

# 2

# Treasures of the Heart

After the news about the coming soldiers had rippled through Biram, the village never quite calmed itself again. Among the adults, I noticed, conversations took on a slightly uneasy edge.

However, the insistent rituals of daily life beckoned. Men went back to their fields and herds, leaving the village square to the dozing grandfathers. Father went to his orchard. Mother and the other women busied themselves with cooking and baking, stopping in at a doorway here or there to ask for a recipe that might help stretch their family's store of flour, grain, sugar and vegetables to feed the extra mouths. The mothers of Biram were miracle workers when it came to multiplying a little food to feed a multitude. They had to be, for few of them had less than seven children and some had fifteen or more.

As for us children, our main job was to go to school and study. Since few of the adults in Biram could read or write, our education was of great importance.

In the week that followed Father's announcement, I bounded off to school with an eagerness that never ceased to surprise my parents. I had loved school from the first day.

But I never slipped out in the morning without a ritual inspection by Mother.

Stepping into the doorway with an earthen bowl cradled in the crook of one arm, she barred my hasty exit. With the heel of her hand—the only part that wasn't already coated with flour—she smoothed my thick dark hair. She had been up since daybreak, mixing together something delicious. One day it was a confection called "circles," rounded sugarcakes flavored with anisette. Another morning it was bread dough. Lifting my chin between a floury thumb and forefinger, she would smile. "Elias, you're a good student. I'm very, very proud of your schoolwork. Be good in class today, won't you?"

Then Atallah, or one of the others who had been impatiently waiting for me in the yard, would poke his head inside urgently. "The bell is going to ring."

"Better hurry," Mother would say, "or Abu 'Eed will be upset."

We hurried through the streets, meeting up with cousins and other bands of children on the way, until we burst like the hordes of Asia into the churchyard just as the huge bronze bell began to ring. The first four grades, which included my class, met in the parish house. The men of Biram had built it with their bare hands out of the ever-plentiful supply of fieldstones and clay. The walls were thick and squat, meeting at odd angles, with huge open windows that peered out on the valleys and let in every stray wind. We were all proud of our school, just as we were proud of the lofting church across the small courtyard, which the people of Biram had also built stone by stone. Pride overruling modesty, they had named the church Notre Dame.

With every child in Biram cramped into one small space, quietness, order and obedience were crucial. We were lined up quickly according to grade. Then we marched into the schoolroom under the all-seeing eye of our teacher, Abu 'Eed.

A kind and small man, Abu 'Eed, had a thick beard that bristled out by his ears like a lion's mane. He was the only priest in our village, a bustling occupation, and he also taught us squirming, younger children math, spelling, reading, geography and the Bible. Since priests were allowed to marry according to our custom, Abu 'Eed had a rather large family, and his gentle fatherliness made him a favorite of mine. If, however, a student foolishly upset the delicate order that held rein on potential chaos, his eyes flashed fiery above the black beard.

It was Abu 'Eed who made school a place of new and wonderful ideas that challenged my imagination. The talk about far away lands needled my sense of adventure. The sound of letters rolling off my tongue as I spelled out a new word—all of it excited me.

Yet I was happier to go home at the end of each day—though not, I'm sure, as happy as Abu 'Eed was to see us go—to my *real* teachers. Mother and Father had always taken our education as their responsibility, not leaving it all up to the school or the church. They were convinced that no one could teach us better than they in such important matters as our heritage, culture and faith.

Every afternoon—on those days when I, myself, was not helping in the fields—I would listen for Mother's return. Then I would hear it—the merry, tell-tale signal that gave out her approach. For Mother jingled. As a wedding gift, Father had given her a necklace, a simple chain of tiny brass links, decorated with fish and doves. The fish, which represented Peter's fish in the nearby Sea of Galilee, were cleverly jointed so they swayed back and forth like real fish—jingling, jingling. And the doves, I knew, represented the Holy Spirit as it had lighted upon Jesus at His baptism in the Jordan River. Mother loved that necklace and wore it always.

When she saw me, Mother would say, "Elias, come here. I found something for you today under one of the stones in the field." Those stones! Our lives were so rooted to this land that the stones even found their way into our play. It took someone as gifted as Mother to transform the backbreaking work of clearing stones into a game, a way of teaching.

"I found a story," she would say with a tired smile. "Would you like to hear it?" No answer was necessary—I was already in her lap. Mother's stories were always rich and beautiful, spinning out of her uncanny memory.

Though Mother could not read or write, she had only to hear a story or poem once or twice and it belonged to her. She knew by heart many of the long epics of Arabic literature. Stanza after stanza, she would weave the tale of some prince or sultan, holding me on her lap as some tragedy or romance or comedy poured out.

The stories she loved best and told with the most vividness, were those from the Bible. Her words set my imagination soaring. I heard the *snap-and-whizz* of David's slingshot as he toppled the giant Goliath; felt the roaring Red Sea split and heave aside in towering waves, letting Moses and the people escape the Egyptian chariots; and I envisioned the dark, lovely, perfumed Queen of Sheba bearing exotic gifts to the foot of Solomon's gold and ivory throne. Mother had chosen to name me Elias—a variation of Elijah—after the fiery prophet who was fed by ravens. Each story formed a familiar footpath of sounds and images in my head. Yet, only one man in the Bible fully captured my awe and love.

The stories about Jesus were, to me, the most wonderful and alive. Jesus, in my young mind, was a flesh-and-blood hero who may have walked the dusty roads into our own village. Mother said He had come to Galilee first, to our hills and our people, after His temptation in the wilderness. It was from His lips that we first heard the good news: God and man were reconciled. Perhaps some forefather Chacour had eaten bread and fish miraculously multiplied by Jesus' hand. Maybe a Chacour boy or girl felt the brush of His fingertips when He blessed the little children, or watched as He healed the sick and the blind. These wonders were real to me, for they had occurred on streets and in homes like those I saw every day.

For instance, I could picture vividly the New Testament story of the men who could not squeeze their paralyzed friend inside a crowded house to meet Jesus. The Lord, as I pictured Him, was seated inside a simple Galilean home just like ours with two rooms and a loft where children slept. In the cold months meals were cooked and eaten in the largest room where children played and guests were welcomed. There were two doors. One led out to a stable where cows, donkeys, goats and chickens were kept in winter. The other led to a small room behind the house used to store hay for the animals' winter feed. Its wooden tiles were easily removed so the hay could be pitched in from the outside.

Jesus, as an honored guest, would have been seated against the rear wall of the house next to the storage room. So the men were not rude, but clever, when they removed the roof tiles and lowered their paralyzed friend right down to the Master's feet. Jesus, of course, had honored their faith and healed the man's stiff, useless limbs. In my imagination, the miracle could have happened on the very spot where Father often rested in the evening, his back against the cool stone.

In this way Jesus became the hero of my whole, real world of stones, sparrows, mustard plants and vineyards. I could easily imagine Him stopping at our house or walking with his disciples through the cool shade of Father's fig orchard.

What Mother treasured most dearly were the words Jesus

spoke to a crowd of Galileans on a hill very near to our house—the hill that Mother loved—the Mount of Beatitudes. The Beatitudes were, to Mother, the very essence of all Jesus' teachings, like the rare extract of a perfume. I would sit on her lap, quietly fingering the doves and fishes of her necklace, listening to the strangely beautiful words:

> "Blessed are the poor in spirit,
>     for theirs is the kingdom of heaven.
> Blessed are those who mourn,
>     for they will be comforted.
> Blessed are the meek,
>     for they will inherit the earth.
> Blessed are those who hunger and thirst for
>     righteousness,
>     for they will be filled . . .
> Blessed are the merciful,
>     for they will be shown mercy.
> Blessed are the pure in heart,
>     for they will see God.
> Blessed are the peacemakers,
>     for they will be called sons of God.
> Blessed are those who are persecuted because of
>     righteousness,
>     for theirs is the kingdom of heaven.
> Blessed are you when people insult you, persecute
>     you and falsely say all kinds of evil against you
>     because of me. Rejoice, be very glad, because your
>     reward in heaven is great, for in the same way they
>     persecuted the prophets who came before you."

*What did He mean?* I puzzled. *How can you be blessed— or happy—if you are poor or in mourning—if someone insults*

*or persecutes you? How can you be hungry and thirsty for
righteousness? What is a peacemaker?*

These things were a mystery to me. What I understood
about Jesus, what attracted me, was His strong, sometimes
fiery nature: the way He erupted into the temple courts,
driving out the greedy merchants and scattering the coins of
the moneychangers; His habit of helping the crippled and
blind, even if He broke the laws and offended the overly-
pious religious leaders. Sometimes I thought He was the
only one who could understand a small boy who also threw
himself into situations—somewhat blindly—a boy whose
tongue sometimes got him into trouble, too, like the time I
committed a capital crime in Abu 'Eed's classroom.

The older students were struggling with a difficult mathe-
matical equation one morning while Abu 'Eed turned to us,
his first-graders, for simple addition. He spewed out several
numbers and asked for a quick sum. Most of the heads were
still bowed, pencils scratching and erasing, when my cousin
Charles shot up his hand. Mine shot up a split second later.

Abu 'Eed nodded to Charles who announced his answer
proudly: "Eight."

"No, Charles," Abu 'Eed replied, shaking his head.
"Check your work more carefully."

I waved my hand desperately, bursting with the right answer. When Abu 'Eed called on me, I blurted, with a smug
look at Charles, "*Nine. The right* answer is nine."

Abu 'Eed smiled at me and was about to give another set of
numbers. But I could not bear the temptation. Charles was
usually a faster, better student, and now it was my turn to
gloat. Foolishly, in a stage whisper that ricocheted off the old
stone walls, I hissed, "See that, Charles? You're a donkey!"

The quiet, contained classroom split open with laughter.
Abu 'Eed strode toward me, like a storm blown up from the

Mediterranean, thundering for silence in the room. His stinging chastisement left me teary-eyed and embarrassed in front of everyone. Even worse, I was afraid that a wagging tongue—in the mouth of who knew which brother, cousin or aunt—would report the incident to Mother and Father.

When school was out, I fled from the mossy courtyard and ran all the way to Father's orchard. The quiet orchard was my special hideaway, my sanctuary where I often went to pour out my small, troubled heart. And who else could I pour it out to but my Champion, Jesus? If Mother's stories taught me anything, it was that He cared for us and He was always eager to listen.

I waded in the cool grass beneath the fig boughs, telling Jesus with all sincerity, "I didn't mean to upset Abu 'Eed. And I didn't mean anything bad when I called Charles a donkey. It just came out . . ." Was He listening? Did He care?

A peculiar stillness seemed to engulf the orchard, although a breeze was rustling the leaves. A sudden sense of awe swelled inside, a feeling of majesty and holiness and—what was it? Friendship. My heart skipped. The sense could hardly have been more real if Jesus Himself had physically fallen in pace beside me.

I simply went jabbering on, imagining the understanding smile. The sense of His presence, the possibility that He had time to listen to my troubles, did not seem at all unusual. So many times before, I had sought Him in my orchard retreat, or in the hills, and there poured out my childish dilemmas, that it seemed most ordinary. Imagined or real, I cherished these times. For then, unknowingly, I first discovered the slim, strong thread of inner peace.

I was thankful that my classroom blunder was not reported to Mother and Father—not that time, at least. Deeply repentant, I hoped I might learn how to harness my tongue.

While Mother captivated me with her Bible stories, Father was the one who forged an unbroken chain of history that led from Jesus and His followers to our own family. Like Abraham or Noah in the Old Testament, Father wanted to be sure his children knew their rare and treasured heritage. After all, our family were Melkite Christians. We were not like some weed newly sprung up after rain, but our spiritual heritage was firmly rooted in the first century.

Night after night, Father would gather all of us under the open stars or around a low fire as the winter wind beat at our door. For the thousandth time he would carry us back through the dim ages with his brilliant histories. I loved every delightful word.

After Jesus' crucifixion, we learned, the flame of His Spirit continued to burn brightly in our villages—though our ancestors were forced to meet in secret for fear of the religious leaders. James, the brother of our Lord, became the spiritual overseer of the believers in Jerusalem.

Not very long after James and the other apostles died, the Church was split, nearly destroyed by a creeping, cultic darkness. A certain group, the Gnostics, claimed that Jesus was a mystical being, and not a man at all. Just when it seemed that these false teachers, would scatter the flock like wolves, the King of Byzantium, newly a Christian, took a strong stand on the side of the early apostles, asserting that Jesus was the God-Man; He had bridged the chasm between God and mankind, bringing peace when He took on our frail, human nature. My family, among many others, sided with the king. Their angry detractors dubbed them with the derogatory name, "Melkites"—or "king's men"—"melech" being the Arabic word for "king." It was these early Melkites who united the splintered churches.

Our Melkite family belonged to a spunky group, it seemed. Many centuries later, after the Crusaders fought bloody wars to implant the influence of Rome in our soil, the Melkites stood firmly against such foreign authority. They remained a separate group of believers, holding to the simple, orthodox teachings of the early church, which angered several popes. Several centuries later, the Melkites built bridges of reconciliation with Rome. This ability to reconcile opposing powers seemed to be an historic hallmark of our Church fathers.

Should Father stray from the familiar trail, all of us would clamor for the *whole* story. One part we loved, with that strange, gruesome tendency of children, was about the horrifying fate of a certain Chacour generations back.

In the 1700s, a cruel Turkish sultan named Jezzar Pasha spread his rule over our land all the way to the Mediterranean. When he took the city of Akko on the seacoast, he decided to raise a fortified wall against foreign warships. Its design called for secret labyrinthine escape routes through the enormous stones. One Chacour was among those forced to work on these sea-walls. While the last bit of mortar was still drying, Jezzar Pasha rewarded them for their backbreaking labors: every one of the builders was buried alive beneath the wall. And so the sultan's defense secrets were guarded forever.

This was Father's most effective way of teaching us two things. First, we should love and respect our Galilean soil, for our people had long struggled to survive here. We were rooted like the poppies and wild, blue irises that thrust up among the rocks. Our family had tilled this land, had worshiped here longer than anyone could remember. And second, our lives were bound together with the other people who inhabited Palestine—the Jews. We had suffered together under the Romans, Persians, Crusaders and Turks, and had learned to share the simple elements of human existence—faith, reverence for life, hospitality. These, Father said, were the things that caused people to live happily together.

Father told his story unvaryingly. At seven, I did not understand much of it, to be sure, but it fascinated me.

And Father taught us something even more valuable than our colorful history. He taught us, in a quiet, subtle way about character. Whether I knew it or not, many of the attributes I imagined in Jesus, my unseen Champion, most likely came from this other hero in my life.

Whenever Father was wronged, for instance, he handled it in a way that amazed me—and caused me to chuckle. One time, he had traded away a huge number of figs and got a very bad piece of merchandise in exchange. The swindler was long-gone when Father realized he had been cheated. But Father never cursed. With a placid tone, and a wry smile on his face, he said, "May God bless that man—and take him to heaven!"

Father's gentle spirit had an influence far beyond our immediate family. One man that father influenced was a certain Father Maximus, who often visited in our home. Over the usual cup of steaming, thick coffee, he would politely inquire about our family, then probe Father for a solution to some touchy, upcoming debate among the Church heirarchy. He continued his visits after he became *Bishop* Maximus. Later, he would become *Patriarch* Maximus IV, a famous reformer in the Vatican Councils. This great man recognized that Father's opinion was not subject to changes of emotion, or the pressure of other men.

Even news about soldiers coming to Biram with guns could not unsettle Father. Since the announcement of their coming, the soldiers had sent word to the village *mukhtars* that they would stay for only a few days and they would take nothing. They were just looking over the land. Father accepted their word as a gentleman. If need be, these Jews from

Europe could settle in our village and farm the land that lay open beside our own fields.

But my brother Rudah was alarmed at the talk of machine guns. A few days after Father first told us the news, Rudah shocked us all by bringing home a rifle—one of the two or three guns in all of Biram, a rusted antique used for shooting at wolves that came to prey on the village flocks. The wolves were in little danger of being hit.

When Father saw the rifle he erupted in a rare show of anger. "Get it out of here! I won't have it in my house." Mother and the rest of us stood frozen and mute.

Poor Rudah was wide-eyed, stunned. "I—I thought we might need a gun to protect ourselves in case—"

"No!" Father would not hear more. "We do not use violence *ever*. Even if someone hurts us." He had calmed a bit, and he took the gun.

"But Father," Rudah persisted, anxiously, "Why do the soldiers carry guns?"

Slipping his arm around Rudah's shoulders, Father replied, "For centuries our Jewish brothers have been exiles in foreign lands. They were hunted and tormented—even by Christians. They have lived in poverty and sadness. They have been made to fear, and sometimes when people are afraid, they feel they have to carry guns. Their souls are weak because they have lost peace within."

"But how do we know the soldiers won't harm us?" Rudah pressed him.

Father smiled, and all the tension seemed to relax. "Because," he said, "the Jews and Palestinians are brothers—blood brothers. We share the same father, Abraham, and the same God. We must never forget that. Now we get rid of the gun."

It is extraordinary how a voice from our childhood, even one word spoken at a crucial moment, can bury itself inside only to reveal its simple wisdom in a crisis our adult minds cannot begin to fathom. Then our whole life is re-fashioned.

I listened to the exchange between Father and Rudah, and watched as they went out to dispose of the gun. Then the incident passed, was locked somewhere inside me with the other jewels of heritage and faith that Mother and Father had carefully hidden there.

The time was soon coming when I would have little else to hold onto but these treasures of the heart.

# *3*

# *Swept Away*

Early one morning, nearly two weeks after the first word about the soldiers, Biram was still resting, quiet in the mists and growing light of dawn. And then the hillside was flooded with the unfamiliar rumbling of trucks and jeeps. Men in drab-colored uniforms with packs slung across their shoulders filled the narrow streets. My brothers and I watched from a corner of our yard, whispering among ourselves as four or five soldiers strode up to our door. They spoke with Father, who welcomed them, and they lugged their gear inside. For the next week, we were told, the soldiers would sleep in the large room beneath the loft where Mother and Father usually slept. My parents would join us on the roof.

Two details I recall most vividly.

Father had prepared us for house guests—but these Zionist soldiers were not at all like our Jewish neighbors who chatted in the yard with Father over coffee. Not that they were unkind or rude. When Father killed and roasted the lamb, blessing the feast and the men, they politely bowed their heads. Mother served them heaping plates of lamb and vegetables and bread which they ate heartily. But they remained aloof, almost brusque. To my disappointment, the feast turned out to be much less of a happy celebration than I had expected. I sidled up to Mother, feeling shy and uneasy in their presence.

And the second thing I recall was the guns. All the while, my eyes were drawn by their cold glint. They were always present, even when we ate. I noticed the small, carved trigger where the finger would rest, squeezing . . . squeezing . . . the long, sleek barrel . . . the tiny, death-spitting mouth . . . an explosion shook my imagination. I shuddered and looked away.

The guns set us apart entirely, no matter how polite the atmosphere. I understood even then that the guns were might—power—and that my family and the villagers of Biram had no might. In the coming days the guns were everywhere while our life went on as usual. We went off to school and the barrels glinted at every corner. At night we lay down on the roof under the cold, clear-shining spring stars, and the guns were propped beneath us.

After a week, word passed through Biram that the military commander had some urgent business with the men of the village. Father went along to the square, expecting to hear that the troops would soon be moving on. Instead, the commander, a short, bull of a man, had delivered some alarming "confidential news."

"Our intelligence sources say that Biram is in serious danger," he announced tersely. "Fortunately, my men can protect you. But it would risk your safety to stay in your homes. You're going to have to move out into the hills for a few days. Lock everything. Leave the keys with us. I promise nothing will be disturbed."

When Father told us about the order, he reported that most of the village men were disturbed. They remembered the turmoil of the 1930s with the occupying British forces. And there had been word of new bombings in Jerusalem, of

trouble between the British and the Zionists. If there was to
be any confrontation between these forces, the men of Biram
decided it would be best to keep their families safely out of
the way. The commander urged them on, saying, "Travel
light. Take nothing with you. You must leave today—as soon
as possible."

To any other people, sudden evacuation—leaving home
and all the conveniences to live outdoors with a large family—would be threatening if not entirely miserable. For us, it
did not seem so difficult. We were accustomed to spending
entire days outside, and we often slept on the ground when
travel or work among the flocks and fields took us away from
shelter. Then we would simply huddle together beneath a
tree or beside some rocks and be content. Often, as in times
of mourning for a deceased relative when no one cooked, we
relied solely on our land, eating nothing but figs and olives
for several days at a time. Since we children had already been
sleeping on the roof, we accepted it as another part of the
adventure.

Quickly, Mother and Father set the house in order, urging
us to hurry and leave behind everything but the heavy
clothes we were wearing. I was the only one permitted to
carry a blanket with me. Having just been in a scrap with my
cousin Asad, I was allowed to wrap this covering over my
face to hide a black eye which was somewhat painful and
embarrassing. Then we were hurried outside.

Father locked the door behind us. Then he handed the key
to one of our soldier-guests who was leaning against the front
wall, his gun hanging casually from a strap over his shoulder.

"I know that God will protect our house," Father said
sincerely. "And you'll be safe, too."

"Yes," the soldier replied with a smile. That was all.

When we left our yard, I was amazed to see dozens of
people moving through the streets, joining other families and

streaming out of Biram. Father led us down the steep hill-sides, toward a grove of olive trees, with Rudah and Chacour walking manfully beside him. Mother held my hand as I stumbled along, the blanket held protectively over my bruised eye. A woman who had been struggling along ahead of us with a child balanced on each hip had to stop and rest. Now I saw that she was an aunt, one of Father's sisters. At the edge of the grove, I caught a glimpse of my cousin Asad and his family. Our eyes met, and he ducked his head with a guilty look. Then he disappeared amid the hundreds of other villagers who were trekking out of Biram.

Every family seemed to have the same idea: The olive grove would be the perfect place of refuge during our vigil. The crowd spread out beneath the old and twisted boughs that spread for acres and acres down toward the valley. It was said that the trees had grown here since the time of Christ or before. Perhaps He and the disciples had eaten olives from these very branches. Now the trunks were cratered and dark with age, but the fruit was still plentiful and delicious. The silver-shading leaves would protect us from sun and rain. And from here, the men could best watch the comings and goings in Biram on the hilltop far above us.

Living as a nomad would be a great adventure—at least I thought so.

In a day or two, when the pain and swelling left my eye and I was ready for fun, the novelty of camping had worn off for everyone else. My brothers were simply sullen. The men, I could tell, were beginning to feel nervous that they had left their homes and lands under the protection of strangers. The older people were starting to suffer from sleeping on the damp, stoney ground. Though the days were sunny, the temperature dropped rapidly at sunset, plunging us from a hot afternoon into a shivering night. Everyone was thankful that I had brought my blanket. All six of us children would try to squeeze under it while Mother and Father huddled together uncomfortably on the ground.

The cold was somehow bearable. The rain was not. A heavy, gray bank of clouds covered the hills on the fourth day. A chilling drizzle spattered through the olive leaves, soaking the grass, mixing the gravel and dirt into mud beneath our feet.

Father led us through the trees to the grotto at the edge of our land. The inside walls were layered with gray and green moss, and a faint smell of damp humus and of goats hung in the air. It was small, but all of us could fit inside, protected from the night drafts and sudden rains.

For nearly two weeks, the men kept up their vigil, watching for threatening activity in the village. Occasionally, a fleet of trucks would arrive in a cloud of dust, and shortly they would drive out again. Mostly, things remained quiet. The people of Biram continued to camp under the olive trees, foraging for food, drinking from artesian springs and getting stiffer each night from sleeping on the ground. Still there was no word from the soldiers.

At last the elders decided not to wait for the military commander's signal to return. A delegation of men collected in the olive grove and climbed the hill to Biram.

Before long, they came running back, their faces a confusion of anguish and fear. The horror of their report spread through the grove.

Upon entering Biram and passing the first house, they had seen that the door was broken in. Most of the furniture and belongings were gone. What was left lay smashed and scattered on the floor. At the next house, it was the same, and at the house across the street. Chairs were smashed, curtains shredded, dishes shattered against the walls.

Then they were stopped by armed soldiers. The one who

appeared to be in charge waved his gun menacingly and barked, "What are you doing here? Get out!"

Angry, and certain that these impudent soldiers needed a reprimand from their superior, the men stood their ground.

"Where is your commanding officer? We are the people of Biram, and we want to bring our wives and children home!"

The one in charge approached them, his gun held squarely across his chest. "The commander is gone," he said coolly. "He left us to protect the village. You have no business here anymore."

At once, all the men raised their voices.

"Protect our village? You're destroying it!"

"Intruders!"

"Get out—leave us in peace!"

The soldiers leveled their guns at them, flicking off the safety switches. Angrily, one of them growled, "The land is ours. Get out now. *Move!*"

The betrayal cut like a knife. A few of the men were bitterly angry, seething with the thought that we had been tricked out of our village by these European men we had trusted. Others were simply bewildered. Pain etched every face.

Father and Mother seemed as bewildered as children by such a callous betrayal. I think it was simply beyond their understanding.

The poor *mukhtars* were mobbed with questions: "How can we get Biram back?" "What's going to happen to our homes?" "Can't you make the soldiers leave?" Of course they could do nothing—two aging, unarmed and bewildered men against the guns of these soldiers.

More immediate was the need for shelter and protection from the weather. Obviously, we could not continue to live exposed to rain and the cold nights.

After a brief discussion, it was proposed that we climb the next hill to Gish, our nearest neighboring village. Surely the people there, who were also Christians, could made some provision for us temporarily while we sorted out this mistake by the rude, young soldiers.

Cresting the hill that rose between our village and Gish, we felt a strange somberness. No shepherds greeted us as we crossed the open fields. The lot where young boys played soccer was vacant. A frightening pall of silence hung in the streets between the empty houses where young women and grandmothers should have been chattering among sleeping babies and old men.

After a long search through the empty village, we discovered ten elderly people who told us they had been left behind. From them we learned that these unarmed people had suffered a fate similar to our own.

Soldiers had arrived in trucks, they told us. But for some reason, they did not use the ruse with these people that they had used in Biram. With machine guns leveled, they abruptly ordered the people to get out, not bothering to drive off these few old men and women who were apparently too feeble to abandon their homes. One old man was certain that the soldiers were impatient to get the evacuation over, because he had heard gunfire just outside the village, "Just to warn the people to move along faster." Most of them suspected that the villagers had fled into Lebanon, which was only a few kilometers distant.

"We do not know when they will return," said one old man, next to tears.

"Or *if* they will return," added another grimly.

Even with this weight of sadness, they offered us a sort of ruined hospitality: "You are welcome to stay in our village" they told us, "though little is left here."

He was right. The soldiers had rampaged through most of

the homes, smashing or carrying off the furnishings in their trucks. At least it was shelter.

Unfortunately, there were fewer dwellings in Gish than families from Biram. In some homes, two families were cramped into a single room with old sheets or worn carpets hung for dividers. For families with ten or more children, conditions were utterly miserable. Abu 'Eed visited, offering comfort and encouragement.

Father was fortunate enough to find a tiny, one-room house for us. He was also able to find a small room nearby for his aged parents who had suffered terribly during the nights outdoors, as had all the elderly of Biram. Our room was dilapidated, barely larger than the grotto on Father's land, and empty but for a few broken chairs. In one corner I found a smashed toy—a doll with its head crushed in. Fingering it, I thought of the child who must have dropped it in fear and confusion and a ghostly feeling came over me. I drew my hand away suddenly and never touched the doll again.

Straggling groups that had been driven from other villages carried more distressing news as we settled uncomfortably in Gish. The soldiers were moving systematically through the hill country, routing the quiet, unprotected villagers. Many were fleeing on foot for Lebanon or Syria. And there was talk of violence in the south. A certain, unnamable eeriness clung to the air with each fragment of information that came.

We wondered, as we tried to piece our lives together, when the soldiers would return and what they would do if they found us in our neighbors' village. And though Mother and Father repeatedly assured us that we were safe, one thought remained fearfully unspoken: What had happened to the men, women and children of Gish?

I would be the first to learn the answer.

A week or more after our arrival, Charles and I were

shuffling glumly through the streets together when we found a soccer ball. It was slightly soft from the cold, but still had enough life to respond to a good kick. Immediately, Charles broke into a trot, footing the ball ahead of him. "Come on, Elias," he called. "Let's have a game!" From side streets and open doorways, ten other boys joined as we passed.

Dodging through the streets, we reached a sandy, open lot at the edge of Gish. With the innocent abandon of small boys, the fate of Biram was momentarily forgotten. We raced up and down the lot, loosing our pent-up energies in a swift-footed competition.

Charles' team scored two points almost at once. One boy was lining up for another attempt, eyes riveted on the goal, when I charged him, roaring, laughing, waving my arms. He kicked hard, and the ball breezed by my head, high and wild, out of bounds. I pivoted and tore after it. The other team dropped back to defend their goal, and my teammates took their field positions awaiting my return.

I reached the ball where it had thumped and settled in a stretch of loose sand. Oddly, the ground seemed to have been churned up. I stooped and picked up the ball, noticing a peculiar odor. An odd shape caught my eye—something like a thick twig poking up through the sand. And the strange color. . . .

I bent down and pulled on the thing. It came up stiffly, the sand falling back from a swollen finger, a blue-black hand and arm. The odor gripped my throat. . . .

"Elias, what's wrong?" Someone was hollering in the reeling distance.

Numbness dulled all feeling. The stiff arm lay in the sand at my feet—a boy's arm. I imagined the face—sand in the sealed eyes—gagging the slack mouth. I thought I was yelling. No sound could escape my throat. Vaguely, I could hear Charles beside me calling. . . .

Later, the shallow graves were uncovered. Buried beneath a thin layer of sand were two dozen bodies. The gunfire that the old man had heard had done its bitter work.

The victims were hastily re-buried in honorable graves. There was seething anger and talk of retribution. But how could there be any retribution when we had no power against this madness? Most of the men, Father especially, would have no part of such ugly talk.

As for me, the innocence and durability of youth were on my side. No one mentioned the incident to me at all. Mother, Father and my grandparents were overly kind, ignoring my outbursts of impatience or tears. My brothers and cousins eventually distracted me with more games, though we avoided the sandlot for quite some time.

In the coming months, as summer crept into Galilee, I was little aware of events outside our secluded hills. But major decisions were being made by nations far more powerful than ours--decisions that would soon leave us without a homeland or an identity. Father and the village elders honed their disbelieving ears to news about the drama that was unfolding across Palestine and in the world's supreme court of justice—the United Nations.

The elders learned, as news and rumors traveled like wildfire through Galilee, that the "question of Palestine" had come before the U.N. It seemed that the Zionists no longer wanted the British to control Palestine, and they wanted to establish their national homeland in place of ours. The British, whose military and financial ability to govern Palestine were bankrupted by the long war in Europe, could not stop the Zionists from taking over the land. The Zionist forces, known as the *Haganah,* had taken over the munitions factories in the south and were using the mortars, bombs, machine guns and heavy equipment against British and Palestinian alike. Each time a Palestinian village was raided, a few of its men would gather in the hills with their donkeys and antiquated carbines in a pathetic attempt to protect their land. These ill-prepared bands were subsequently crushed by the the *Haganah* in further reprisals. It was hardly a contest. And now the United Nations had been called upon to arbitrate a peaceful solution to the bloodshed.

Certainly, the men of Biram reasoned hopefully, the powerful nations of the world who controlled the U.N. would reach a just solution. The summer of 1947 passed, the rains of autumn soaked the earth, and still we waited as refugees. Month after month in our cramped quarters, we prayed for the news that we could return to our homes in Biram.

In November, refugees fleeing from larger towns brought more devastating news.

Palestine was to be partitioned in what the U.N. called a "compromise." Our elders and hundreds of thousands of Palestinians throughout the land were shocked beyond words, for the terms of the "compromise" were brutal.

The Zionists were to possess the *majority* of Palestine—fifty-four percent—even though they owned only seven percent of the land! In five major areas that were being handed over, well over half the people—up to seventy and eighty, even ninety-nine percent—were Palestinians. The "compromise" gave the Zionists almost all the fertile land, including the huge, main citrus groves that accounted for most of our peoples' export income. It gave away the vast Negev region where the Bedouins produced most of the barley and wheat grown in Palestine. There was three times more cultivated land in this one area than the incoming, European settlers had cultivated in all Palestine in the previous thirty years. [1]

Such concessions, in the eyes of the Palestinian people, could hardly be called a "compromise." Our people were being told to hand over more than half of our well-cultivated lands that produced our only livelihood.

How had such a sweeping and one-sided decision been reached? Among the nations of the world, the U.N. vote was accepted without question or protest.

As an eight-year-old boy, the elders' talk was just words to me. It would be years before I discovered the truth about international intrigues and clandestine agreements that had led to this Middle East tragedy. For now, the eyes of all were blind to these political machinations. And I was only aware that my peaceful homeland of Palestine, known as the Holy Land, had become a land of war.

Shortly after the U.N. vote, the British announced that they would be withdrawing all forces from the Middle East the following spring—by May 15, 1948.

Throughout the winter months and into spring 1948, we heard of more terror, of villages blown up by barrel-bombs while others narrowly escaped the flaming ruins of their homes. Thousands were now uprooted, living in the hills and arid wastelands.

Most especially, we came to fear one name—the highly-trained and single-minded Zionist organization called the *Irgun*. One of its leaders had been among the ten terrorists most wanted by the British for his part in bombing the luxurious King David Hotel in Jerusalem. His name was Menachem Begin and his proclaimed goal was to "purify" the land of Palestinian people.

In April of that year one of these acts of purification was the destruction of a village on the outskirts of modern Jerusalem. The scene at Deir Yassin was later recorded by an eyewitness, Jacques de Reynier, the head of the International Red Cross emergency delegation.

On April 10, Reynier was stopped on the Jerusalem road by members of the *Irgun*, who refused him entry to the village. He bravely pushed through their lines and into homes where he found "bodies cold. Here the 'cleaning up' had been done with machine-guns, then hand grenades. It had been finished off with knives, anyone could see that. . . . As I was about to leave, I heard something like a sigh. . . . It was a little girl of ten, mutilated by a hand grenade, but still alive. . . . There had been 400 people in this village; about 50 of them escaped and were still alive. . . ."[2]

The native Jewish people were shocked and disgusted. In tears, they protested that such things violated their ancient beliefs. Upon hearing the news about Deir Yassin, the Chief Rabbi of Jerusalem flew into a fury.

Unfortunately, religious censure was not powerful enough to stop the military machine.

As May approached, more trucks rumbled into peasant villages. And daily, refugees swarmed through Galilee bringing word of more towns sacked. Others drowned in the Mediterranean as they tried to swim for overcrowded refugee ships leaving from Haifa and Lidda.

Early on May 14, while the last British were scrambling to get out of Palestine, a young man named David Ben Gurion assembled more than two hundred journalists and photographers to proclaim the establishment of the State of Israel. Within hours, the government that the new Prime Minister Ben Gurion and his comrades had been carefully planning for months was in place. Within sixty minutes, the United States officially recognized the new nation of Israel under Zionist rule.

The same journalists and photographers who attended Ben Gurion's proclamation soon recorded for the world our summer of tears. Through May, June and July, almost one million Palestinians were driven out of the newly-proclaimed democracy. Soldiers from surrounding Arab nations of Egypt, Iraq, Syria, Jordan and Lebanon fought to stop the takeover, but were driven back. In the confusion and terror, husbands and wives were forever parted, parents lost small children never to see them again and many elderly died.

The Jews who had been our neighbors, our friends who lived with us and shared our customs, ached for us. They could not understand or accept such violence, but they were powerless to help. And the nations were silent.

By autumn of 1948, the Zionists had swept north and were close to us again. The forces were "cleansing" the towns around the Sea of Galilee, almost at our doorstep. As winter set in—our second winter in Gish—the Zionist advance stopped short of the upper Galilee. Thin blankets of snow fell, and only one question was discussed in low voices around guttering fires: Would the soldiers find us here in our hill-country refuge—or would they think we had fled to Lebanon or Syria or Jordan as had so many others?

Although we had been refugees from our own home for almost two years, Father never prayed for us, for our protection or provision. He continued in his simple belief that his children were like "the birds of the air" that God had promised to feed and he refused to worry over us—though I think Mother had a more difficult time when food was scarce. We had barely survived our first year, eating animals from the abandoned flocks, making bread from the stores of grain and working small gardens.

I was increasingly aware of Father's unbelievably forgiving attitude toward the soldiers. He faithfully continued our times of family prayer and never failed to pray for those who had made themselves our enemies. Night after night I would lean my head against Mother, fingering the fish and doves on her necklace, and hear Father pray: "Forgive them, oh God. Heal their pain. Remove their bitterness. Let us show them your peace."

As spring 1949 pounced upon us, tiger-like with its ferocious heat, I could see little peace anywhere but in our own home. An uneasy lull moved in with the blistering days and cool nights. We rose each morning with the fear that we might not lie down on our mats that evening. At any moment we, too, might be swept away.

On a sultry morning, our lull was shattered.

I was playing in some trees near the road to Gish with a few cousins and some other boys when we heard the ominous, rumbling of trucks. In the distance, rounding the side of the next hill, came the first of the army vehicles. For a split second we looked at each other in wordless terror, then scattered.

When I reached home, Father was in the doorway with Mother and the other children. The trucks had reached the edge of the village, and a harsh metallic voice rang from a loudspeaker: "All men must show themselves at once. Young men and old men. Come outside with your hands on your heads. Do not resist."

I looked at my brothers. Rudah and Chacour were now young men. Musah was a teenager. They, too, would have to go. What about Atallah and me? And what would the soldiers do to the men who surrendered themselves? My face tingled with a burning fear.

Father looked grim, but as he turned to my three oldest brothers he spoke with a perfect calm. "Come, boys. It will be all right."

Wardi clung to Mother, and Atallah and I stood numbly at her side. The four of us watched Father march bravely, with Rudah, Chacour and Musah striding uncertainly beside him, out to a large open lot where the soldiers stood with leveled guns. Atallah and I crept outside to watch. I was shaking, nearly choked with tears.

Crouched in a shadow outside the door, we stared as all the houses of Gish gave up their men and older sons. Among the somber throng we saw all of our uncles, their faces riddled with tension. Young men filled the streets, their eyes a confusion of fear and defiance. Behind them shambled the old men, not willing in their fierce pride to sit at home while their sons and grandsons faced the danger alone. As they came, they were ordered into one large circle that stretched around the entire open lot.

Immediately the soldiers began to accuse. "You are rebels. Tell us where your guns are hidden. We know you are fighters—Palestinian terrorists."

These words scorched me. Father, my uncles, cousins and the *mukhtars*—"terrorists"?

On and on went the interrogation as the heat of the day built to a searing brightness. The men began to squirm, drenched in their own sweat as the sun poured down. There was no water. Neither could they relieve themselves. Without ceasing, the soldiers demanded that they surrender their weapons. There was nothing to give up; there were no guns anywhere in our village. Still the soldiers harassed them through the long afternoon. Men weakened and some dropped as the heat and accusations pounded at them.

We could see Father at the far side of the lot. Sweat dripped from his chin. His eyes were shut and occasionally his lips would move. I knew that he was praying for the soldiers.

And suddenly, as the afternoon sun waned, it was over. The commanding officer barked abruptly: "Go back to your homes. But don't try to escape."

Father nearly collapsed inside our door. He and my brothers rested in the quiet coolness of the house while Mother and Wardi rushed to bring them water and a little food.

As the darkness settled over us, no one dared to light fires or to cook a meal. The soldiers remained in Gish, gathered around their trucks or patrolling the streets. We waited in a misery of silence, hoping they would leave.

Father seemed to have some inner warning of what would happen next. He drew close to each of us in turn, with a gentle touch and an inscrutable look. I suspected that he was praying for us one by one. His eyes looked weary, and yet some reservoir of calm lay behind them. When he smiled at me and touched my shoulder I could almost believe that the soldiers would leave soon and let us live in peace.

And suddenly there was noise and bustling in the dark streets. I shuddered to the sounds of loud angry voices, gun-butts thudding at doors and the growl of truck motors starting.

The loudspeaker was blaring again. "Come out of your houses. We want all men to come out and give themselves up. You are leaving here at once. . . ."

Mother seized Father's arm, sheer anguish carving her gentle face. "Michael, what are they doing? Where—?"

"Katoub," he stopped her, drawing her close. "God is watching us. You have to be strong—" he paused, his voice dropping, "for the little ones."

For a moment they held each other as the terrible blaring continued. The wailing outside cinched the knot in my stomach. Tears streamed down Wardi's face. Then Father turned to my brothers and said quietly, "We'll go now."

Mother trailed after them, kissing Rudah, Chacour and Musah, wiping her tears with the back of her hand. I stood frozen beside her on the doorstep, Atallah and Wardi peering mutely over my shoulder. In the glare of headlights and flares, we stared into the darkness and chaos.

Soldiers were hurrying the men and older boys at gunpoint onto the open-backed trucks. More guards stood at the tail-gates barking orders. In the doorways, women stood weeping, their babies and smaller children wailing loudly in their arms. Father and my brothers had already been jammed onto one of the trucks with several dozen other men, and we could no longer see them.

As the last tailgate slammed shut, the loudspeaker called out to the women. "We are taking your terrorists away. This is what happens to all terrorists. You will not see them again."

And then the trucks were rolling, rumbling away into the night. In the blackness, women flooded into the streets, sinking to their knees and weeping, calling the names of their husbands and sons.

Mother was too desolate to try to offer comfort to any of my aunts who came and hung on her shoulder. She walked numbly inside, and sat holding Wardi, Atallah and me long into the night. I clutched her skirt, shutting my eyes against the wails and screams. For a long time—I could not tell how long—I sat this way. I must have fallen asleep.

When I opened my eyes again, it seemed to me much later. All was silent but for the barking of a dog far off. Silent, but for the inner voices that begged inside us: *Where have they taken my father—my sons—my husband? Will I see them again—or never again?*

I shifted a little and looked up at Mother. In the dark I could not see her face, but heard her slight whispers.

In these, the darkest hours of her life, Mother would turn again and again to her only source of strength and inner peace. She stroked my hair, and continued softly praying.

# 4

## Singled Out

Gish was a world in a dark dream for weeks after the men and older boys were taken from us.

Women moved through the streets and in the garden plots like solemn apparitions. Beneath the longing and sadness, their eyes stared with a frightening hollowness. If the men had been slain before our eyes, I think it would have been easier to go on with living. Women who have lost men at sea, or whose sons have simply vanished in foreign wars understand this feeling. Not knowing is a horror. In the back of each woman's mind, no doubt, during the aching, endless nights, were the shallow graves in the sand lot outside Gish.

Another unknown was disturbing. A few well-armed soldiers were still guarding Biram, yet they did not bother us. Why? Were they just waiting to return any day or while we lay sleeping, and haul us off to—what fate? Along with the emptiness of loss, there burned a certain fear.

Had there been no younger children demanding attention, had it not been for the comforts of Abu 'Eed whom the soldiers had left behind, some of the women might have opened their jaws in one unending scream, stepping into the blackness of the mind from which there is no return. Instead, they were forced into a rhythm of simple duties: childcare, work in the fields, preparing meals.

In all this, an unusual thing was happening to Mother. One by one, other women would come to her. The moment they looked into her eyes, they would fall on her shoulder weeping, broken inside. Instead of dissolving along with them, Mother would offer a listening ear, a few words, and the women would leave comforted. I had seen Mother's own tears, could sense her continuing hurt at the absence of Father, Rudah, Chacour and Musah. But somehow she never seemed alone—never abandoned. She took on a gentle strength, and to anyone around her it gave the solidness of hope.

Mother's greatest comfort was in prayer. As the weeks wore into months, and evenings lengthened with the coming of summer, she continued to gather us around her outside under the deepening skies. To Wardi, Atallah and me, it gave certain peace to carry on Father's custom. To Mother, peace came not from habit or ritual words, but from talking to a dearly respected Friend—One who cared for us. Like Father, Mother spoke to this divine Friend in simple words, never doubting for an instant that a loving ear attended her voice.

With a solemn innocence, she prayed one evening, "We know that you watch the sparrows, Lord. And only you know where Michael and the boys are this night. Will you watch them for us? Guide their steps? We give them into your hands."

In my mind's eye, I could picture Jesus. He was looking at Mother with tears in His own eyes, drawing from her the hurt behind her brave words, leaving a solidity of spirit in its place.

"Allow us to be your servants here in Gish," she continued. "Let our hands be your hands to comfort the suffering. Let our lips bring the peace of your Spirit."

Something was happening to me during these months, too. More and more, I came to enjoy solitude. In the middle of a game I would stop, very often staring up into the hills. Then I would quit the group and wander off alone, followed by the questioning glances of my playmates. The last wild irises and poppies, anemones in yellow, pink and scarlet were pushing up between the stones. In a week or two, the hot breath of summer would burn the slopes a brittle brown.

The morning after Mother's special prayer, I climbed alone to the top of a hill and sat beneath an olive tree. To the south somewhere beyond the hills, rocked the Sea of Galilee. I imagined my Champion striding toward me over the storm-churned waves, calming the waters with a word: "Peace." I thought of Him climbing the Mount of Beatitudes. There, as Mother taught me, He said, "Blessed are those who mourn for they will be comforted."

What did these words really mean? For the first time, I turned them over and over in my mind like a smooth stone. Almost without thinking, I began innocently pouring out my heart. "Mother has your comfort. I can see that. But can't you just speak a word and make all this trouble go away? Do you want *us* to be your lips and hands and feet—as Mother prays—to bring peace again? If that's true, you can use my hands and feet. Even my tongue," I added, thinking of my usually fiery words.

I didn't know it then, but this was to be one of the most important prayers of my life. And a first, small step committing me to a long journey.

At the moment, I was thinking about Father and my brothers, slipping in one special request just for me. "Please bring them home," I whispered. Then I wondered if Father would have called that a selfish prayer. I should leave such matters in God's hands, Father would say.

Three months passed, and still we had no word about the men. The matter of our own safety loomed over us as the summer of 1949 stretched on. In nearby Biram, the soldiers were strangely quiet.

One evening, after prayers, Mother allowed Wardi, Atallah and me to play outside as usual until bedtime. But at dark, she hurried us inside, for few remained outdoors then. After she settled us in bed, Mother moved about quietly in the dim light of a candle or two finishing her chores for the day. The very last sound I heard each night before drifting into sleep was the metal *click* of the heavy door-bolt, our only earthly protection from unwelcome visits in the dark.

A sharp elbow woke me. Atallah was plumping his pillow and fidgeting beside me. He was having a hard time settling down. I could hear Mother preparing for bed. Still groggy, I was about to push Atallah's knee out of my back when a noise disturbed the quiet. Atallah and I both sat up, suddenly awake, listening. Mother and Wardi sat listening, too.

The sound came again and drew my eyes to the door. The bolt rattled in its lock. Someone was trying to open it. A muffled voice from out in the night hissed, "Let us in. Quickly. Open up."

I shrank back against Atallah, wide-eyed. Fear ran a cold fire up my spine. Mother had risen to her feet and stood frozen, one hand over her heart.

"Who is it?" she called bravely, but her voice shook.

"Let us in. Hurry . . ." the voice hissed again and was drowned out by others as the rattling continued.

"Go away," Mother called. Now she was next to tears.

"I say it's Michael. Let us in. We're home."

"Michael?" Mother almost shrieked.

Atallah and Wardi and I were at her heels as she hurried to

the door, slamming back the bolt. With our wits gathered, there was no mistaking that voice. Mother threw open the heavy door.

Four men pushed inside with the dark draft. I startled for a moment, as if we had been tricked and these were strangers crowding in before us in the flickering candlelight. They were very thin—almost emaciated—their cheeks sunken behind unkempt beards. Their clothes were dirty and ragged, and the worn shoes were nearly falling off their feet. In the eyes of my three brothers was a wary, hunted look. Only Father seemed as calm as if he had just spent a pleasant day in his fig orchard, though he was obviously exhausted.

Mother threw herself on them, hugging, holding, kissing them, laughing and weeping with inexpressible joy. Rudah, Musah and Chacour, who at any other time might have shown the reserve of young men, began to weep and hug everyone—even Atallah and me.

I threw my arms around Father's waist. "Hello, Elias," he smiled, gently stroking my tousled hair. "I see you've taken care of everyone while I was away."

Mother was hurrying about getting food and water. She was wringing with questions. "How did you get back here? Did anyone see you? Where did the soldiers take you? Are the other men with you?"

We sat long into the night, Father's arm around my shoulders as he answered her questions. They had come on foot, of course. No, they were not seen since they had traveled mostly at night. I watched his serene face, and it seemed a miracle to me that he and my brothers were alive and sitting close beside us as the candles burned low. Most amazing was the story of their survival.

On the night they were taken from Gish, the men were driven through the dark for hours. It was cramped and cold and windy in the trucks. They had passed Tiberias on the Sea of Galilee, so Father knew they were headed south. But where? Toward daybreak, he saw that they were nearing the hill country that rose up to Jerusalem. The trucks pulled off the road north of the city near the town of Nablus on the border between the new State of Israel and the kingdom of Jordan. Hopefully, it was the soldiers' intent to drop them across the border—and nothing worse.

As the men staggered from the trucks in the bleak light of dawn, the soldiers opened fire, aiming just above their heads. The men of Biram scattered in terror, running like wild men in every direction. Some fell and were almost trampled. Father and my brothers tore through the open fields, stumbling through bushes and over stones. At last they distanced the shouting soldiers and the rifle fire, which was meant to drive them from their homeland for good. But Father and my brothers had only one plan in mind from the first moment: They would find their way home again, or die in the attempt.

Gradually, they made their way to a road that seemed to angle in a northeasterly direction—first toward Amman, then toward Damascus in Syria. They had no idea where any of my uncles had gone, and only occasionally did they find other men from our village on the road. Many of them were too frightened to consider returning to Gish. Most frightening was the treatment they received at the hands of other Arab brothers in Jordan and Syria where Father hoped to find help and the customary hospitality. At the first town they came to, Father and my brothers were turned away as vagabonds. Our "brothers" it seemed had no compassion for "dirty Palestinians." At the next town it was the same, and the next. They were driven out like lepers. For days they walked with little or nothing to eat, forced out of every town. At times they were so desperately hungry that they grovelled in the dirt for insects to eat. Nights they spent in abandoned animal shelters in the hills or sleeping in the dirt and grass to wake soaked with dew and shivering. Had it not been summer, they would surely have died.

For days and weeks they traveled until they were close to Damascus. Then Father struck a southwesterly route that would carry them through a corner of Lebanon and into northern Israel. Once he spotted Mount Meron, the highest mountain in all Galilee, Father knew he was home. When they reached the fields outside Gish, they waited until dark in the event that soldiers were stationed in the village. Then, furtively, they crept through the streets until they found the right door, unsure that they would find us here after all their hardship.

Mother almost blushed when Father teased her about her stalwart refusal to open the door to her own husband. And he held her close. Three months of torment were over at last.

As Father prayed with us that night, I leaned against him, basking in the richness of his deep voice—I had missed it so much—and I was almost too overjoyed to comprehend his words.

"Father," he prayed, "they are treating us badly because we are the children of Ishmael. But we are true sons of Abraham—and your children. You saved Ishmael from death in the wilderness, and you have saved us. You brought justice for him and blessed him with a great nation. We thank you now, for we know that you will bring justice for us. . . ."

In the coming months a few more men would return. One day, a certain village house would be somber, with a mother and her babies facing the uncertainly of life on their own— and overnight, joy would dawn in that home again. Yet for every family that was reunited, many more never saw their husbands, sons, fathers, uncles and cousins again. Mother and Father had both lost several brothers, and some of my older cousins had simply vanished as well. Only rarely did

we hear some word—and no one could judge its reliability—
that this uncle or that one was living in a refugee camp in
Lebanon or Syria.

For the rest of that year I lived with a lingering shadow of
fear that the soldiers would surprise us one day, roaring in
with trucks to drag away the men once more. This time,
perhaps, they would finish off their job more forcefully.

The soldiers never did raid Gish again. In fact, as 1949
came to a close, the new government seemed to undergo a
strange, confusing reversal in its push to drive out the Palestinian people entirely. The elders began to hear that the
agricultural settlements were actually hiring Palestinian men
and boys—a few at a time and "unofficially"—to work at
menial jobs. Later we learned why. A cheap work force was
crucial to the survival of their newest *kibbutzim,* since many
of the incoming settlers had lived their lives in European
cities and did not know how to farm. Now we understood
why the soldiers never came back to drive out the men who
had returned, for they were skilled in agriculture and desperate to work, even for low pay, to support their large families.

Something else was happening behind the scenes in the
new government of Israel, though the village elders had no
way of knowing it yet. Soon they would see strong evidence
of internal struggles within the government, clues that this
new nation—which the whole world was proclaiming a
"modern miracle"—was actually rife with factions vying for
power.

Early in 1950, as the cold spring rains swept the hills,
flooding the wild wells and driving our meagre flocks of
sheep and goats into sheltering grottoes, more heart-stop-
ping news reached us.

Plans were underway for a new *kibbutz,* an experimental,
agricultural community set up by the new government for

settlers from Europe and America. It was to be located just across the fields from our still-empty homes, and strangely, it would be called Biram also. More startling was the news that some of the fertile land surrounding Biram had been sold to new landlords who had emigrated from foreign countries and were living in nearby Jewish towns. Now we understood why the soldiers had stayed on in Biram to "protect" it from our return.

Most painful was the word that Father's fig orchard had been purchased from the government by a well-to-do settler as some sort of investment.

At this news, Father's face furrowed with grief. I was terrified that he would weep. He was still, his eyes shut, his mustache drooping above a faintly trembling lip. He had planted those fig trees himself one by one, straining with heavy clay jars of water up the steep slopes, caring for each sapling until it was strong enough to survive on its own. They were almost like children to him.

And in the same moment, I wished that Father would rage. Perhaps fear had numbed my anger before this time. Now as I watched Father's pain-lined face, I shook with a horrible feeling. Wardi and my brothers squirmed. None of us could bear to see Father—dear, gentle, Father—in such agony of spirit.

When he spoke in a few minutes, his voice was barely above a whisper.

"Children," he said softly, turning those sad eyes upon us, "if someone hurts you, you can curse him. But this would be useless. Instead, you have to ask the Lord to bless the man who makes himself your enemy. And do you know what will happen? The Lord will bless you with inner peace—and perhaps your enemy will turn from his wickedness. If not, the Lord will deal with him."

I could scarcely believe it! His life's work had just been torn from his hands. His land and trees—the only earthly possessions he had to pass on to his children—were sold to a stranger. And still Father would not curse or allow himself to be angry. I puzzled at his words to us.

*Inner peace*. Maybe Father could find this strength in such circumstances. I doubted that I could.

I am certain that Father had a strong voice in what happened next. Immediately after the distressing news, the remnant of our village elders convened and decided to submit a petition to the new Israeli Supreme Court of Justice. In short, the petition welcomed the settlers to the new Biram. What had been taken could be considered as a gift from our people. However, they asked, could we return to our homes in the old Biram to live peacefully beside our new neighbors and farm the remaining land?

Father's other response to the sale of his land was more of a wonder to me.

In a few weeks we heard that the new owner of our property wanted to hire several men to come each day and dress the fig trees, tending them right through till harvest. Immediately, Father went to apply for the job, taking my three oldest brothers with him. They were hired and granted special work passes, the only way they could enter our own property.

When she heard what Father had done, Mother stared at him incredulously. "How can you do this, Michael? It's so awful. So wrong."

Father replied simply, "If we go to care for the trees, we'll do the best job. Someone else won't know what they are doing. They'll break the branches and spoil the new growth." This was something Father could not bear to think.

And so, three years after our expulsion from Biram, Father and my brothers were hiring themselves out as laborers—just for the chance to touch and care for Father's beloved trees. I did not know the word *irony* then, but I could understand pain.

For months the elders of Biram continued in the hope that

the new government would allow them to return to their homes. However, among the younger men, this hope was not so strong. A few began to speak of moving to the coastal cities of Haifa and Akko where, they had heard, Palestinian families were clustering in hopes that their men could find factory jobs. The new Israel was struggling to westernize, and that meant rapid industrial development. Again, lower-paying jobs were opening to Palestinians a few at a time. Of course there was deep resentment. But living would be better there, the young men argued—at least they could feed and clothe their children. Here and there, a family moved out of Gish, shrugging off the elders' assurances that justice and our return to Biram were imminent.

Daily, as summer ripened, Father and my brothers hope-fully climbed the long hill that separated Biram and Gish to tend our own trees for the new landlord. And each day they would report on the progress of the new Biram *kibbutz*—a dwelling going up here or there, poles being uprighted for the telephone and electrical wires, the constant surveillance by police from the nearby towns and the arrival of the first foreign tenants. Father bore, with characteristic patience, the indignity of having his special worker's pass scrutinized by the soldiers several times each week before he could set foot on what had been his own land.

In this lull, terror would single me out.

For us boys, one of the few diversions from this chancey and unpredictable adult world was still a game of soccer. It was almost a daily ritual. Though I was spending more and more time walking alone in the hills, I still loved to rough-house with other boys. At eleven, I had become quite fast, though my kicking aim was not always so accurate as the older boys who mostly made up the teams. Atallah and Asad stuck up for me if there was ever a question of leaving me out, and I was a wiry and eager player.

We were lost in a fierce competition on a hot afternoon toward the end of summer. I watched the ball being footed up the field, passed from one teammate to another, when a sound caught us by the ears. Heads spun around. Everyone stopped dead in their tracks, the ball trailing off forgotten. It was a sound we feared by instinct.

Cars were speeding into Gish. My heart, pounding from the playful activity, nearly stopped. Were they again coming for Father and the other men?

Several dark automobiles and jeeps raced into view, billowing clouds of dust in their wake. At the edge of our playing field, close to where a few of us were standing, they braked to a sudden, unexpected stop. Most of the other boys were running for home, Atallah and Asad with them. They must have thought I was right behind. In confusion, three or four of us stood transfixed, as if freezing in place would keep us from being seen. As the vehicles halted, a dozen men burst onto our playing field.

"You! Come here!" A huge man yelled, striding toward me. I could see by his uniform that he was a military policeman and, like the others, he had a gun at his belt. Roughly, he grabbed me by the shoulder, his fingers digging painfully. The other boys had been seized also.

"What shall we do with them?" shouted my captor.

I tried to twist out of his excruciating grasp, not that my shaking legs could have run if I'd wanted to, but the iron grip of his fingers dug into my neck.

"First you tell us what you did with the wire," my captor demanded, shoving me against the other boys. A wall of men surrounded us, firing questions and accusations.

"Who put you up to it? Tell us that."

"You don't want us to go after your families, do you?"

"Maybe you'd care to tell us where the terrorists are hiding in your village."

"I think they want a beating."

I struggled to hold back hot tears. The others stared, mute with fear. None of us had any idea what they were talking about. Somehow I choked out a few words.

"We don't know what you are saying. What wire? We don't know about any wire. We've been playing soccer. . . ."

"*Lies,*" one of the men barked. "All you know how to do is lie."

For what seemed an endless time, they continued to threaten and badger us. First one, then the other would scream at us, always coming back to the charge that we had cut some kind of wire. Over and over, we protested that we had no idea what they were talking about.

By this time, our teammates had sped through Gish breathlessly spilling the story that we were being held. People were flocking to see what had happened. In the crowd of men, women and children that were clustering some distance from us and the knot of angry men, I could see Mother. Father was striding toward us, his face a mask of fear. His coming, I hoped, would mean our rescue.

"What are you doing with these boys?" he challenged them as boldly as he dared. "What have they done that you're treating them like criminals?"

"They cut the telephone wire that was being run up to the new *kibbutz,*" one man declared. "It was strung along the ground, waiting to be mounted on the poles. A section has been cut. It's missing. These boys were seen cutting it, and we want to know who put them up to it."

It was obvious that they had simply grabbed us, the first children they saw, and we were to be the "culprits." I suppose they thought that by threatening us, our parents would surrender the true villain. Unfortunately, there was no one to surrender.

"You think you can get away with terrorist actions?" One of the men glared at the crowd, picking up a stick. The others searched the ground for sticks, too. "I think your boys will have some information for us if we coax them."

The men closed in on us, their bodies forming an impenetrable wall. I huddled against another boy, looking desperately for a way of escape. The huge man who had first grabbed me raised the stick over his head.

A stinging *crack* seared my shoulder. I drew a sharp breath and tried to shield myself from his next blows. The boy beside me screamed as he was struck across the back. We tried to fend off the slashing sticks with our arms, which only infuriated our captors. Another whipping blow stung my bare legs just below the short pants I was wearing. Then another. Two across my back—lashes like hot brands. Above our own cries, I could hear women begging the men to stop the beating.

As they struck us, the men shouted at our horrified families: "You are worth nothing—and your children are worth nothing. You are doing underground work. Your children are thieves and you're the ones who teach them to steal!"

I thought the whipping would never end. And then, suddenly, the huge man grabbed me by the shirt.

"Now bring that piece of wire to me," he growled in my face. Then he shoved me away.

I stumbled toward Father on shaking legs, still stinging and choking on sobs. In confusion, I blurted, "Father, where do I go?"

The man, thinking, perhaps, that Father had cut the wire, turned on him with a face distorted by anger.

"Is this what you teach your son?" he erupted. All the men were shouting and cursing. They swore at Father, calling him, among other disgusting things, that degrading name with which we were to be branded—"dirty Palestinians." I was shocked, pained more deeply than by any physical bruises, that my gentle father could be so abused in front of our whole village by these crude men.

Yet Father bore their insults silently.

The huge man doubled his fist in Father's face. "Tomorrow we'll come back" he promised, "and you give us the wire or you and your son will come with us."

Still glaring at us, the policemen stalked back to their cars and jeeps and drove off.

The very next morning they did return, shoving Father and me into an automobile. As we rocked and jolted down the rough roads to their station in a nearby town, a chilling thought tempted me to tears: *I will never see Mother again. They will throw me in jail and forget me.* And at the same time, another voice spoke from deep within my thoughts, soothing me with the words, *Peace, be still.*

For many hours, the police interrogated us, hinting that I was in for a terrible time if Father did not help them find their wire. He remained calm, a study in politeness and respect despite their angry questions, firm in his assertion that I was innocent. In disgust, the police finally gave up and drove us back to Gish. When they left us, there were no more threats, but I feared that the incident was not to be dropped.

That evening, Mother called me to sit beside her when everyone else was outside and we were alone. Now that my arms and legs had begun to stretch long and slender, I could no longer sit on her lap. I leaned against her, her bright kerchief soft against my cheek. Gently she took my hand.

"Elias, I want to give you a treat," she said softly. "I have saved an egg, and I'm going to cook it for you." For us, struggling to get by on the barest amount of food, a cooked egg was indeed a treat. This was Mother's special way, I supposed, to help me feel a little better.

She hesitated for a moment, then continued. "But first,

Elias, please tell me . . ." she faltered, "tell me where the wire is. Bring it to us, and then this trouble will be over."

I sat up stiffly and stared at her. She was no longer young, the struggle of caring for a large family under such poor conditions had lined her face. A wisp of hair—graying hair— had escaped her kerchief. A certain weariness showed through her sweet smile. Poor Mother, after all the terror she had faced—the disappearance of Father and my brothers, many members of her own family driven into exile—I could not be angry with her. She simply feared the loss of her youngest. But I was angry—and hurt that such terror tactics could cause her to doubt her own son.

"Mother, I didn't do it." That was all I could reply to her.

For the next few days I drew away from my family and my playmates, retreating into the sun-parched hills to be alone. But not completely alone. The sheep on the hillside, the twisted, ancient olive trees, the far-off blue hills of the Golan Heights that towered around the Sea of Galilee—all these things reminded me of my constant Champion. My pace quickened up the brown-burnt slopes as if He were walking right beside me at that moment. I could almost see His understanding look, and in my head I heard Him, repeating the words Mother had quoted to me hundreds of times: *Blessed are you when people falsely say all kinds of evil against you . . . for in the same way they persecuted the prophets who were before you.*

I shook my head as if arguing with a playmate. I did not want to hear these words. I was no prophet. I only wanted to know why I was being singled out for such horrible treatment.

I had forgotten my prayer of months before when I had asked Him to use my hands and feet and tongue to bring peace back to our peoples' hearts. Had I remembered, I would not have understood then that such a commitment, when spoken from the heart, means being called out, singled from the crowd. It may mean drinking from the bitter cup of rejection and humiliation—standing in the face of the lie in order for the truth to win out ultimately.

I only knew that, despite my anger, I wanted things to be put right so that I would never again hear the wail of village women grieving for their lost—never again see the hurt in Mother's eyes, or hear Father cursed. I wanted so much for us to live in peace with our Jewish neighbors as we had before the soldiers came. The thought of living the rest of our lives in fear was stifling, and as I trudged through the cedars and the scattered olive trees, I wondered what Jesus would do.

Unknown to me, someone had an eye on my daily wanderings.

One afternoon I returned home to find Father working in his small garden plot, hoeing up the dry, spent vegetable plants. He saw me coming, stopped and leaned on the long, wooden handle. Thinking I might disturb his work, I was going to pass by. He stopped me with a question.

"What do you do in the hills, Elias?"

I paused, wondering if he would think it odd if I answered, "Talk with a Friend." After a moment's thought, that was my reply.

Father nodded, his eyes scanning the hills, a faint, mysterious smile on his lips. "I thought as much," was all he said. Then he went back to work.

I walked away, and the moment passed. It would be some time before I realized the importance of that brief encounter. For Father was a man of deep insight and wisdom, and a plan for my future was already turning over in his mind as he churned the stiff soil.

By the end of the week, the question of my guilt or innocence was resolved. We learned that a wagondriver, returning to the new Biram *kibbutz* with supplies, produced the missing length of telephone wire. It fit exactly in place between the cut ends. He had run over it with his loaded wagon and the wire had sheered off between the metal-rimmed wheels and the rock-hard ground. He had carried the section away with him, planning to return it on his next trip.

We never received any apology from the police, and I was only too happy to let the entire episode be forgotten. And shortly, in the closing months of 1950, we received joyous news from the Supreme Court of Israel that temporarily wiped the incident entirely from our minds.

An official letter arrived in Gish, postmarked in Jerusalem. The elder's hands fairly shook with excitement as he read it aloud. The letter said we could return to Biram immediately by order of the Supreme Court! Hurriedly, with great rejoicing, plans were made for the move home.

While the women were gathering up the few things they had acquired in our three years of exile, some of the elders crossed the hill to Biram and there displayed our letter to the soldiers.

The commanding officer shook his head. "This letter means nothing to us. Nothing at all. The village is ours. You have no right here."

Though the elders argued with him, he would not honor the order. They were turned away.

For the first time our elders realized that something was seriously wrong within the new government. They already had ample evidence that these Zionists were not at all like our peaceful Jewish neighbors. The new Israel seemed to be a nation where the military ruled, ignoring the will of the country's judges and lawmakers, powerful enough to do whatever it wanted. The elders were devastated by this revelation.

Upon hearing the soldiers' refusal, I saw the pain in Mother's eyes, felt the ache in Father's heart for his lost land and fig trees. As Christians, they would accept their lot. Yet I could see the joy draining from their lives. And still rumors of violence whispered through the hills, bloodshed and terrorism everywhere in the land.

Were there only two choices left to us—surrender to abuse or turn to violence?

As for me, the beating had forced me to stare into the face of this frightening question. What choice was I to make? And as my twelfth year approached, I was soon to take the next step on the journey that would lead me to a third choice—one that my Champion made so long ago in these same beautiful, fought-over hills.

# 5

# *The Bread of Orphans*

Early in 1951, the elders agreed to petition the Supreme Court a second time. In their letter of appeal, they explained the Zionist soldiers' defiance of the court order. Again we would wait in hope for many months, innocently believing that the Court could somehow make the military obey its legal decisions.

Though we would receive a surprising answer, I would be far from Gish when it finally came.

On a hazy, humid morning, our Bishop arrived in Gish. He had been tirelessly visiting all the outlying villages arranging for deliveries of food, clothing and medical supplies. Along with the list of urgent needs, he was accumulating a lengthy accounting of complaints.

He walked the streets of Gish, escorted by crowds of men who pointed out the overcrowded houses, the children playing in worn and too-small clothing. Gradually, their complaints turned to the loss of property—twelve acres, twenty, thirty, forty—each man topping the next as they bemoaned their confiscated land. Though they tried to contain their anger in respect for the Bishop, they were soon tirading loudly about the losses sustained. Again and again, the men tried to pin him moth-like with one pointed question: What power did he have to get their land back?

Father was walking along quietly at the edge of the crowd. In a lull between the complaints, he spoke up.

"Bishop, excuse me. I have a request also."

The Bishop knew Father well from occasional visits to Biram in the past. Possibly he expected another listing of wrongs and injuries. He nodded politely, with a hint of weariness in his smile. "What is it, Michael?"

"I have a son—my youngest. His name is Elias," Father explained. He's a good student, and I want to send him to a good school. Please, can you help me?"

The other men were jolted by the abrupt shift in conversation. Impatiently, without thinking, they interrupted. "What are you talking about? We're trying to get our homes and our land back. And you're bothering the Bishop with something like this?" As soon as the heated words were out, they flushed with embarrassment.

The Bishop's smile broadened. "Let me think on this for a little while, Michael. Come and see me before I leave the village." And then the crowd swept him along again.

Father kept the promised appointment with the Bishop. Though he did not have a proper school to send me to, the Bishop explained that there was an orphanage near his own home. I would be welcome there, and the bishop promised to see to my education personally.

Father accepted the offer at once with deep gratitude. Eagerly, he discussed his plans with Mother and found her less eager to send her youngest child—her favored son—so far from home. In the end, of course, she submitted.

Then Father took me aside. There was a slight catch in his voice as he explained, "In a few days, we will take you to the bus. You are going to Haifa on the coast to study with the

Bishop. This is a wonderful opportunity for you, Elias. You will never have such a chance here in Gish.

"And there is another thing," he said, pausing. Now Father searched my eyes with his steady, serious gaze. "You are not being sent away to be spoiled by privilege. Learn all you can from the Bishop. If you become a true man of God—you will know how to reconcile enemies—how to turn hatred into peace. Only a true servant of God can do that."

I could scarcely fathom such an enormous-sounding task. I only knew that the prospect of life in Haifa sounded thrilling. At twelve years old, I had never been beyond our hills.

On the morning of my departure, I was awake with the earliest light. Even so, Mother had awakened before me, had finished her silent prayers, and was packing a small bag with my few belongings. Rising from my straw mat, I felt uneasy. In the stillness of dawn, I heard the faint jingle of the doves and fish on Mother's necklace—and suddenly I did not feel at all adventurous. An emptiness opened in the space below my ribs. I could only pick at the special egg Mother had so lovingly saved for my farewell breakfast.

The whole family trudged together to the bus stop—at a crossing of roads not far from Gish where the bus occasionally found its way. Mother and Father were to accompany me to Haifa. Wardi and my brothers followed glumly, barely looking at me all the way to the bus stop.

And then the ancient bus lumbered up, its bitter-smelling exhaust tingling my nostrils. My bag was loaded, we climbed on board, and Father carefully counted out the coins for our fare from what he had earned by working in our orchard. Without ceremony, the bus jolted forward, rumbling down the hills. We rounded a bend—and my brothers and Wardi disappeared. With a sick feeling, I realized suddenly that I did not know when I would see them again.

"Seventy-five kilometers to Haifa," the driver shouted over the roar of the bus. The few other passengers merely nodded. To me that was an unimaginable distance—impossibly far! I sat between Mother and Father, picking at the torn seatcover, miserably jouncing with each bump. An empty, rootless feeling—one I'd never felt before—widened inside me with each passing kilometer. Mountains and towns and orchards sped by our window, and only one thought filled my head: *How can I ever find my way back home again? Where is my home?*

Unknown to any of us, I was about to face the most crucial turning points, confronted at such a tender age by events and choices that would shape my entire life.

When we stepped off the bus in Haifa I was completely bewildered. The huge station was a mass of busses, autos and travelers. The men and women standing in the ticket line wore the nicest suits and dresses I had ever seen. Their clothes seemed stunning compared to the scuffed shoes, baggy shorts and shirt I had gotten through the Bishop's relief efforts. And I could not stop craning my neck, scanning the buildings and clustered homes that covered the low, rolling hillside down to the shore of the Mediterranean Sea.

Somehow, Father guided us through the busy streets—paved streets!—to the correct address. With each corner we turned, the buildings got older and more decrepit until we reached the Bishop's orphanage—a squat, gray-looking building jammed between the others.

On the doorstep we were greeted by a young, plain-looking woman with a lilting European accent and a welcoming smile. Inside, the Bishop received us, chatting with Father, and I knew this was a great honor. Mother judiciously eyed the accommodations, nodding politely as she met the other Belgian and French ladies who, in service to the church, lived here with the orphans.

Before I knew it, Mother and Father were out on the doorstep again. A quick hug from Mother—and she turned her face away. A wave from Father whose smile seemed a little fixed.

Then they were gone.

The young woman gently laid an arm across my slumping shoulder as I stared dejectedly for a time into the empty street. "Come, Elias," she said tenderly—if unthinking. "I want you to meet our other orphans."

The European ladies immediately swooped me under their collective wing, fussing over me like so many mothers. Though they were tender and caring, the deep homesickness left an empty gap in my stomach. I was a country boy, uprooted from quiet and replanted in a noisy city, my roots pinched beneath concrete. My move to Haifa had caused me to miss home—our real home in Biram—more than I had during our exile in Gish. How deeply I missed walking alone in the hills, drinking from the clear-water springs of Galilee. Amid the busses and grimy buildings of the city, I had to force my mind from those faraway hills. During each long, grueling lesson, they beckoned to me with a wild freshness that was suddenly missing.

And in the Bishop's rigorous schedule for me, I began to lose something else. Studying the Bible as if it were a textbook was very unsatisfying. The sense of Jesus' presence, whether real or imagined, had always been so vivid. In Haifa it seemed like memory of a bygone childhood. I clutched at the New Testament promise Mother had so often quoted: "I will never leave you nor forsake you." Despite those words, I was lonely. I longed for the days when I had felt His presence in the wild places. I longed for solitude.

For several months this yearning ached in me, deep as a prayer that coursed through my whole being. And then I was surprised by an unexpected "gift."

It was bedtime. I was curled up in an over-stuffed chair in a
corner of the common room which we used both for study
and play. Spread across my lap was one of the huge,
gloriously colorful picture books the housemothers had
brought from Europe. The other children were busy with
games as I leafed through the pages, escaping into a fantastic
world of adventure. One of the housemothers, a French
woman who was preeminently observant of the rules, came
in and announced the end of playtime.

"Come, Elias," she said crisply, taking the book from my
lap. "Into bed."

Another housemother—one whose gentleness and delicately scented lavender cologne made her a favorite of us
all—had also come into the room. She noticed the look of
discouragement on my face. Perhaps she sensed something
beyond a typical, youthful unwillingness to go to bed. As the
last boy filed out of the room, she came to my defense.
"Don't you think we could let him stay up a little longer than
the others? After all, he's a good student. And see how he
loves the books. I'm sure he'll be quiet and not disturb
anyone." She finished with a conspiratorial glance at me.

So it happened that I was allowed to stay up longer than the
other children—all by myself in the common room! It was a
small measure of solitude, not the wilderness peace of Galilee, but it would do.

Once I'd been given this glorious gift, I did not waste a
moment on storybooks. I found an empty journal and began
to fill it with letters to Jesus. I was too self-conscious perhaps
to speak to Him right out loud in a house full of people as I
had in the deserted hills of home. So night after night I spilled
my heart across the blank pages with childlike innocence and
dawning maturity.

*"Mother says you have a purpose in everything,"* I wrote.
*"But I don't understand what you want from us. Is it your*

*plan that Mother and Father suffer as you suffered? Father
will not fight to get his land back as others are willing to do.
Is this the kind of 'peace' you want us to show the world? Will
anyone hear our cry and help us."*

Many nights, during the fall of 1951, I scrawled out my
dearest hope that the Court would order the military to allow
my family and the other villagers to return to Biram. That
ancient village with its moss-covered walls and sheltering
trees seemed to me a cradle of all that was good and simple
and innocent. It was a home that had protected us. The
church that was its living heart had nurtured our spirits. If
only we could have it back. It was all I wanted.

And so, with my nightly writings, I firmly established a
lifelong practice of private communion that proved as vital as
the blood in my veins or the breath in my lungs. It was a
practice established in irony, for at the very moment I tightly
grasped my thread of inner peace again, the seeds of bitterness were about to be sown in my heart.

Christmas passed. In the orphanage our observance was
joyful. If I was still homesick, the simple European touches
added by our housemothers helped to cheer me. More mar-
velous was the sense of holiness, the solemnity and wonder I
felt at the Bishop's Nativity celebration in the huge, cathe-
dral-like church. The bells, the happy carols, the stone arches all warmed me with thoughts of home. In fact, being in
church had come to feel like being at home to me, somehow. I
loved it.

One cold Sunday morning early in January 1952, I was
huddled with the other children in the chilliness of the old
church. We stood to sing a hymn and I turned to whisper
something to the boy next to me. From the corner of my eye,
I spotted him—and my head jerked around. In the back, in a
baggy, worn coat, sat my oldest brother, Rudah. But it could

not be! Why would he come so far? It must be good news about Biram.

In response, he nodded faintly. My mouth must have dropped open in amazement, for one of the housemothers nudged me and gave a stern look. I could do nothing but fidget through the rest of the service, sneaking secret glances over my shoulder to be sure Rudah would not disappear.

When it was over, I broke from the group and ran down the long crowded aisle to him, the housemother calling after me.

"Rudah!" I threw my arms around him. I had grown some, and now we were nearly the same height. "I've missed you. Why are you here? How are Mother and Father? Can you stay to lunch?"

"Come outside, Elias," he said quietly. "I have something to tell you."

On the church steps we paused. I drew my thin coat close to my chin to block the bitter wind. Rudah faced me now with a look of deep anguish.

"Mother and Father sent me to tell you the news. They didn't want you to hear it and worry about us. Elias," he said, fighting back tears, "it was horrible. The soldiers. The bombs—"

"What are you saying?" I pressed him anxiously. Suddenly I was shaking with cold and nerves. Numbly, I listened as the story spilled out.

Some time in early December the Court had again granted the people of Biram approval to return to their homes. For the second time, the village elders marched across the hill and presented the order to the Zionist soldiers. This time, the elders were pleasantly surprised.

Without question or dispute, the commanding officer read the order. He shrugged. "This is fine." And as the elders stood in stunned silence he added, "We need some time to pull out. You can return on the twenty-fifth."

On Christmas! What an incredible Christmas gift for the village. The elders fairly ran across the hill to Gish to spread the news. At long last, they would all be going home. The Christmas Eve vigil became a celebration of thanksgiving and joyful praise.

On Christmas morning, broken gray clouds rolled across the upper Galilee, and the still air was crisp and cold. Bundled in sweaters and old coats supplied by the Bishop's relief workers, the villagers gathered in the first light of day for the march to Biram. Though they were ragged looking, their spirits were high. Mother, Father, Wardi and my brothers all joined in singing a jubilant Christmas hymn as they mounted the hill. It was the first time in nearly six years that such joy had flooded those ancient slopes.

At the top of the hill, their hymn trailed into silence. The marchers halted uncertainly. Far below them, Biram was surrounded by Zionists tanks, bulldozers and other military vehicles. But this was December 25, the morning they were supposed to return home. Why were the soldiers still there? In the distance, a soldier shouted, and they realized they had been seen.

A cannon blast sheared the silence. Then another—a third. The soldiers had opened fire—not on the villagers, but on Biram! Tank shells shrieked into the village, exploding in fiery destruction. Houses blew apart like paper. Stones and dust flew amid the red flames and billowing black smoke. One shell slammed into the side of the church, caving in a thick stone wall and blowing off half the roof. The bell tower teetered, the bronze bell knelling, and somehow held amid the dust clouds and cannon-fire. For nearly five minutes, the explosions rocked Biram, home collapsing against home, fire spreading through the fallen timbers.

Then all was silent—except for the weeping of women and the terrified screams of babies and children.

Mother and Father stood shaking, huddled together with Wardi and my brothers. In a numbness of horror, they watched as bulldozers plowed through the ruins, knocking down much of what had not already blown apart or tumbled. At last, Father said—to my brothers or to God, they were never sure—"Forgive them." Then he led them back to Gish.

I could not absorb Rudah's words. He told me that another village, Ikrit, had also been bombed at about the same time. I was simply cold.

Cold as we parted, hugging on the doorstep of the orphanage. Cold as I picked at my supper in silence. The housemothers did not press me to do my schoolwork that evening, for they had heard the news from Rudah, too.

Alone that night, I was frightened by my own thoughts. I did not know how to handle the anger. More than anger. Rage. The bombing was worse than any physical beating I could have suffered. I could not face my journal, ashamed to pour out my dark feelings there. I lectured myself, wishing that I could be just like Father, who was my indelible example of spirituality. But I was me—a young man with a growing awareness that the world seemed bent on my destruction.

So it was that I buried my feelings, denying the anger that was too ugly to admit. And in that moment a small gap began to widen inside me, an internal battle that I would one day have to reconcile.

In another week, I lost myself again in the journal, posing questions to which I had not the vaguest answer.

*"How can we ever find again the peace we used to share with our Jewish neighbors?"* I wrote. *"How can I help my parents—my Palestinian people?"*

Though I wanted to leave Haifa—to share in the hard life of exile with my family—I would remain for two more years. I was being prepared for the next step on my journey, a step that would carry me farther from home than I could have imagined. It was Father's wish that I study, and I would obey. The Bishop's house of charity would shelter and instruct me.

As with all the people of Biram, I would continue to eat the bread of the homeless and the orphaned.

# 6

## *The Narrowing Way*

The bombing of our homes was a sharp blow that knocked the wind and spirit out of the people of Biram.

In the scant news I heard from Mother and Father came reports that a few more families were leaving Gish each month for the cities. Perhaps they would be better off hidden among the poor masses in a large city than perched on the open hilltops of Galilee. Understandably, they no longer wanted to stand by the elders in their continuing appeals for the return of our land. With the bombing, they had despaired.

Unbelievably, Father and my brothers continued caring for the fig trees in our confiscated orchard, which had escaped bombing. I pictured Father walking stoically past the ruins of our house. Rudah had said it was nothing but a tumble of stones and charred beams. Father, I knew, would keep his eyes and his heart set on one thing: tending the fig trees—at least for a little while longer. Silently he would plod on, hoping that his sons would follow him in bearing the cross of persecution. It was all he knew to do. Even as I admired his courage, I detected in Father a growing twinge of hopelessness. For the first time, I think, I realized that my father was human, a man with weaknesses and a limited understanding of this bewildering conflict in which we were embroiled.

As for me, I entered my second year of studies in Haifa with great listlessness. I had been away from home more than a year, and that nagging, rootless feeling left me empty. Because I was not an orphan, I was never fully accepted by the other boys. This, my early adolescence, was a bad time to be hit with so many crushing blows to my self-worth. A sense of loss—a deep mourning—threatened to cripple my spirit.

Once again, it seemed that I was not to be forsaken. In my loneliest moment, I was given the gift of a special friendship.

During the first week of classes that fall, two new boys came to study at the Bishop's school. They were Faraj and Khalil Nakhleh, and they came from a fairly well-to-do family in Ramah, another village in Galilee where there was no longer any school.

From the first moment I met Faraj, the older of the two, I sensed a special quality about him. He had a certain politeness, a joy, something quite rare that I could not touch, and yet it felt familiar. He was thirteen also, and the first thin wisps of mustache shadowed our upper lips. Though he was about my height, he was thinner, and I tended toward broad shoulders, a barrel chest and angular bones. He had a quick, easy laugh and the ability to draw me out of my grayness of spirit. Even under the heavy load of lessons, there remained a flicker of fun in his eyes. Such an immediate bond sealed between us that I, rather than Khalil, might have been taken for his brother.

What most amazed me was Faraj's unusual sensitivity.

Once, when we were taken as a group to swim in the nearby Mediterranean, I drew apart from the splashing playfulness. The other children were used to my occasional solitary habits. But Faraj appeared at my side, sticking close as I trailed along the hot sand. He listened quietly, nodding and studying my face as I rambled over my confused thoughts about the plight of our families and our own future under the new government.

"What do you think will happen to us?" I pondered aloud.

"I don't know, Elias," he replied. "We can't go to university, that's for sure. They aren't accepting—" he stumbled over the words—"aren't accepting *our kind*."

I knew he meant Palestinians. "So what do you plan to do when we're through here? Work in a factory?"

He stopped. A sweep of white foam raced up the beach and splashed warmly over our bare feet. "I'm not sure," he said in a moment. "But I believe that someone will take care of us. That much I know."

Who did he mean? The Bishop? I wasn't sure what his vague answer meant, but did not pursue it.

At the moment, I needed to be alone to think. Faraj had somehow developed, in a few short weeks, the uncanny ability to read my moods. If he was boisterous and fun-loving, he was also sensitive. He left me to wander and trotted back down the beach to where the others were playing in the crashing waves. I found a quiet spot and sat watching the restless surf, imagining that the great swells were the hills rising around Biram.

Biram that lay in ruins.

The home and church—those two "cradles" that had taught me about the Man of Peace—now in ruins. Destroyed by the violent.

In that silence of spirit, sitting before an eternity of blue sea, a vivid image flashed before me. An image of Biram resurrected beneath the ancient olive trees, of all the ransacked homes restored and the women safe within. Palestinian and Jew—sipping coffee together again in tranquil conversation. The church was rebuilt. Each man, woman and child was like a stone—a living stone—in the rebuilt village.

For a split second, it all seemed so real—so *possible*—that my heart leaped.

Then the image was gone.

Shouting at the far end of the beach shook me from my thoughts. Three or four boys had plunged into the surf. With arms flailing, they raced while those on shore cheered. Now I could see that the one about to take the lead was Faraj. All the girls were cheering him on, which made me smile. Our interest in girls was just dawning, but Faraj was the one whose charm was already landing him in one brief romance after another. I felt a sudden surge of brotherly admiration for him.

I got up and shuffled through the sand to rejoin the group. Faraj had waded up onto the beach again where the others clapped him on the back. His chest heaved as he caught his breath, and his lips were parted in that handsome smile the girls loved. The victor.

Faraj would be a success at whatever he chose to do—at school, in business. He was that sort of boy. And his family had a bit of money. Maybe they would send him to America when he was old enough. And me? What would I do?

Throughout that year and into 1953, Faraj and I grew closer together, sharing late-night secrets when we ought to have been asleep, and studying in the same classes. My grades, in fact, were quite high which pleased the Bishop. Occasionally, he would mention to me a minor seminary he was planning to open in Nazareth, a school for young men who were seriously considering service to the Church. It would be ready to receive students the following year, in 1954. Since I would then be fifteen, he thought I was old enough to be considered.

In the fall of 1953, on one of my very rare visits to my family in Gish, I mentioned the Bishop's offer to Mother and Father. They were subdued when they met me at the bus, still grieving over the recent deaths of both my grandparents. Father, now in his fifties, had finally stopped tending the fig orchard. It had become too emotionally draining, and this heaviness showed through his usual, easy smile. But at the suggestion of seminary they both brightened a little.

"And what do *you* want to do?" Father asked.

I was about to reply, but stopped in mid-breath. It suddenly occurred to me that the decision was up to me. Three years before, it had been Father's decision that sent me to Haifa. Suddenly, I felt that I was stepping through the opening door to manhood, free and trusted and mature in the eyes of my father. I could not answer him just then, but my way was slowly becoming more clear.

Shortly after my return to Haifa, I was summoned to the Bishop's office. I knew what his question would be—and yet I was in for a surprise.

When I reached his office door I paused, and he beckoned me with a wave of his hand. "Hello, Elias," he said, seated behind his desk. "Sit beside your friend."

I entered and was amazed to see Faraj sitting in one of two straight, wooden chairs in front of the Bishop's desk. We exchanged surprised looks as the Bishop began to address us.

"You've both had some time to reflect since I last spoke with you," he said, his kind penetrating eyes moving from Faraj to me. "Now I want to hear your decision. Are you willing to study in Nazareth, and further consider a life of service to the Church? Elias," his eyes riveted on me, "what is your decision?"

I opened my mouth and heard myself answer: "Yes. I want to study in Nazareth."

Without waiting to be asked, Faraj spoke up. "Yes. It's what I want, too."

I could not believe it! Faraj, who was so popular, so charming and such a leader—I'd had no idea that he was considering a contemplative life within the Church. I would have thought it of his brother Khalil—he was sometimes quiet and meditative. And yet I felt at once that Faraj's choice was right. He was so kind toward others, so keenly sensitive. Somehow I had mistakenly thought that his light, good humor excluded him from interest in spiritual things, as if anyone who wanted to serve God had to be an unhappy drudge. I certainly didn't think of myself in those terms.

The Bishop was still speaking, though now he was staring down at his hands which lay folded on the desk. "I will be honest with you boys. It is not an easy life. It requires obedience to God and to your superiors. In Nazareth you can see what it will be like. It's a challenge I extend to you."

He continued talking to us for a few minutes, telling us about our soon-coming transfer to Nazareth. I was hardly listening. Faraj shot me a quick wink, and inside I was about to burst. If the minor seminary would be a challenge at least Faraj and I would face it together.

Our transfer to Nazareth, early in 1954, marked another sharp turning point for me. Distinctly, I began to feel that my path was carrying me into the service of the Church. Strangely, this was both comforting and disturbing.

On the afternoon of our arrival at the new school, St. Joseph's Minor Seminary, Faraj and I were shepherded into a still-unfinished dormitory by a gray-robed brother. As we marched behind him, I noticed that our accommodations would be far less homey than the orphanage in Haifa. The unglazed windows were not even protected by curtains, and a brisk wind blew steadily through the room. It gave us a sharp view of Nazareth, sprawling over the valley below us— the presumed site of Mary's well and Joseph's carpentry shop. But the room was like ice. I might have known then that our days of warm nurturing by the housemothers were really over. Though life in the orphanage had been regimented out of necessity, for order and convenience, the priests and brothers at St. Joseph's would soon impress us that the rule here was regiment at all cost.

As the brother left us to stow our few belongings beside our newly assigned beds, he said brusquely, "You are expected at prayers soon. Be sure you are not late."

We settled our things, bantering and joking with the few other boys who had arrived before us. There would be just thirty-four students in all that first year. When it was time for prayers we bounded to the church that stood beside our dormitory. Noisily we burst through the entryway and were halted immediately by a stern frown from one of the brothers. Tiptoeing, we slid noiselessly onto a bench near the back.

Up at the front of the sanctuary, a brother was reading the Bible aloud in a rich, sonorous voice that echoed through the dim vastness. The last light of day edged through the windows, warming the stone-gray interior with a certain, faint glow. I glanced up at the high-vaulted ceiling, and drank in the exotic scent of incense that hung in the air. A deep silence seemed to engulf even the voice of the brother—the wonder-filled silence of eternity.

I felt a familiar thrill. To me it was like the comfortable silence between friends, a moment of quiet when nothing needs to be said—when you simply dwell in the warmth and joy of each other's presence. Yes, that's what I felt—that familiar *presence*. The hushed and worshipful atmosphere was drawing from the wells of memory in me. I was bathed again in the wilderness peace that had steeped the hills of Biram. I was reliving, in a split second, those endless days when it seemed that I was actually walking alongside my childhood Champion, Jesus. Unmistakably, I felt a rush of joy stirring in my spirit.

I sat in this inner silence, swaddled in the feeling that in this place—this church, this very bench—I was *home*. Here, in this *presence*, I had dignity again. I thought of the words of Jesus which Mother had loved to repeat time and again: *"Peace I leave you. My peace I give you. Not as the world gives. . . ."*

Now I thought I understood the longing for solitude that had become so clear in Haifa. It was not a call to abandon humanity—but a heartcry to stand alone before God. And alone with Him I could find perfect serenity. It was so comforting. Surely this was what Father had intended when he first sent me off to be trained by the Bishop. For me, the service was over too soon. I wanted to bask in the stillness forever.

As we started into our rigid school schedule, I searched for spare moments when I might slip away into the engulfing quietude of the church. There I felt close to the Father-heart of God. Many times Faraj would join me, which I did not mind at all. I enjoyed his company, for, even when we were in the middle of a hectic day or studying for a test, he seemed to carry inside him a rare tranquility. And when we sat together in the rich quiet of the church's interior he was perfectly still. Sometimes I would open one eye and watch him. Without so much as a fluttering eyelash, he sat as if sculpted in deep contemplation.

Once while we were alone in the church, he opened his eyes and caught me watching him. He grinned at me, with that charming smile that lit up his dark eyes, and he said, "You feel Him, too—don't you?"

I was surprised. I had thought that the overshadowing presence was mostly a product of my own childhood. I did not expect the feeling to be shared by anyone else.

Apart from our visits to the church together, I began to experience a most unusual phenomenon on my own.

Many nights I would curl under the covers on my bed,

listening to the rhythmic, slow breathing of the other students until I dropped off to sleep, too. Then, some time
around midnight, I would wake up as if I had been shaken by
someone. I would blink into the darkness, and my first
thought while swimming up from the ocean of sleep was
always the same: *Come to the church.* It could not have been
more distinct if Faraj or one of the others were whispering in
my ear.

One such night, several months after our arrival in
Nazareth, I rose and dressed quietly. Then I slipped out into
the mysterious and cool-moving airs of midnight. A bright
moon had risen, nearly full. I entered the still sanctuary
where a silver radiance glanced off the stone pillars. The
glow seemed to mirror and gather high above me near the
vaulted ceiling, drawing my gaze upward. I slipped quietly
onto a bench, still shaking myself awake, absorbed in the
beauty of the chill and echoing sanctuary. I expected to find
the joyful solemnity that so often met there.

That night I felt uncomfortably on edge.

While the moon cast shadows about me, my thoughts
turned to memories of Mother and Father. Of course I
thought of my family often, but this night I felt something
stronger than mere sentiment. In the quiet spaces of my
heart, I seemed to hear a voice repeating familiar passages
from the New Testament. It had been nearly eight years since
I last sat on Mother's lap listening to these beautiful phrases
pour from the treasure-store of her memory. Now they were
not just memories, but burning words. I found myself stuck
on one passage: the Beatitudes.

As a boy I had sometimes thought them enigmatic, though
they had comforted me. Suddenly they were terribly disturbing. Why did they sound so embarrassingly contradictory?

How could you be meek and inherit anything in this power-
hungry world? And if you tried to live in happiness and

peace, wouldn't someone just kick you out of your home, bomb it and sell off your land? What did it mean to hunger and thirst for righteousness? Were the Beatitudes impossibly beyond reconciliation—uttered by Jesus merely to exercise pious young scholars?

I was amazed as these questions—gentle but provoking—barraged me. They almost seemed to be coming from outside my own thoughts.

My eyes traced the curve of an arch until it disappeared in the blackness above me, and the irony of my situation struck me: I had just found, in my midnight ventures to the church, a haven of tranquility—only to have it disturbed by this growing inner restlessness. Why was this thread of inner peace always being stretched to the breaking point?

I had stayed in the sanctuary too long, wrestling with my thoughts when I should have been back in bed asleep. All at once, I felt greatly exhausted. Instead of getting up immediately, however, I sprawled across the bench, pulling my jacket tightly about me, and tried to shut off my turbulent mind which had gone somewhat hazy with fatigue. Maybe if I laid still for a few minutes the disturbing thoughts would go away. Then I would slip back to the dormitory. I closed my eyes to rest them, just for a minute. . . .

Someone was shaking me by the shoulder. Not the gentle shaking that had seemed to wake me at midnight, but a rough, insistent hand. I blinked. The rose glow of early sunlight colored the stone walls. I looked up into the frowning face of one of the brothers.

"What are you doing here?" he demanded.

I sat up stiffly, a little dazed, hardly knowing what to reply. "I came to be alone. To pray. And I guess I fell asleep."

He seemed not to hear. "You are supposed to be in the dormitory—not out wandering in the night. There is no excuse for this."

I was stunned. Didn't he believe me? I tried to protest: I was not wandering. Nor was I making up an excuse.

In response, he lifted me by the collar. As an adolescent I was almost the same size and height as he, but I never thought to resist. "Come. We're going to the principal," he said, shoving me ahead of him.

The principal, Father Basilios Laham, was normally a kind, if somewhat strict man. This morning he peered at me questioningly from across his desk. Quickly my story tumbled out. I had gone to pray, that was all. Surely I had done no harm. Somehow I failed to impress him as a saintly, young visionary.

"I'm sorry, Elias," he replied gravely. "You have broken the rules. What would happen if we allowed every student to do just as he wished? As I am bound by the laws of the Church, so you are bound by the rules of the school. You must be punished."

For the first time, I stood face-to-face with the unbending rules of the Church as an institution. I could not understand why strict obedience to a rule was more important than a heart seeking God. Unhappy though I was, I could not fault the principal. He was just a man carrying out his job to the best of his ability. In the end I submitted, more or less quietly, to my punishment: forty days of restriction.

Unfortunately, this would not be my last exposure to the side of the Church that seemed to have forgotten the humanity it was intended to serve. Unfortunately, too, my quick tongue, which had so often gotten me in trouble as a small boy, had only gotten quicker with adolescence. On one occasion, I was sentenced to forty days of silence for disagreeing with the brothers. I wanted more Bible study and less sports activities. I was judged insubordinate and unsubmissive.

My timing was especially bad at the most obvious moments.

One day late in 1954, we were informed that the Archbishop was coming to inspect our school. Accompanying him on this visit was a very distinguished foreign dignitary, the new Ambassador from the United States to Israel. The Bishop would be coming from Haifa to be with them, eager, of course, that the very best impression be made. Our dormitory was to be spotless, and we were warned again and again to be impeccably polite.

About a week later, in the middle of a morning lecture, there was a loud knock at the classroom door. Father Laham swept into the room along with the Bishop, the Archbishop and the Ambassador. The brother who was lecturing paled slightly, looking almost as gray as his robe. Nervously he brushed chalk dust off his fingers and extended a trembling hand to greet the dapperly dressed Ambassador. The Archbishop, who took special pride in knowing each of prospective seminarians by name and by village of origin, began introducing us one by one. As his name was called, each student would hop to his feet, bowing his head respectfully.

After several introductions, the Archbishop turned to me and smiled warmly. I was on my feet at once. "This is Elias Chacour," he announced broadly. "He is from Gish."

"Sorry, Archbishop," I spouted without thinking. "I'm not from Gish. I'm from Biram."

Suddenly everyone was staring at me. Even Faraj, who was used to my outspokenness, gulped. The brother, the principal and the Bishop colored in unison—though the Ambassador smiled and did not seem to notice my indiscretion. One never corrects an Archbishop.

"Biram does not exist," the Archbishop snapped piquantly. All his warmth was gone.

Bristling, I announced loudly, "But I have hopes it will exist again one day." I could not allow the suffering of my people to be erased so blithely, even in respect for an Archbishop.

"Sit down!" he ordered, gritting his teeth.

After a brief, somewhat stiff chat with the poor, fidgeting brother, the visitors swept out of the room and on to tour the rest of the school. I hoped my comment would be forgotten—but no. Later I was treated to a prolonged tongue-lashing for "insolent remarks."

Alone in the dormitory, I chastised myself for not keeping a closer guard on my tongue. Why did this stubbornness persist about Biram? After all, the Archbishop was right in one sense—it *was* destroyed and our land confiscated. What was it that refused to let me forget—to brush it aside as the Archbishop did? He was a man of God after all. I wished I could be more like him—or more like Faraj who was so agreeable. I vowed that I would try to be more quiet, more respectful and obedient to my superiors.

On one hand I felt this growing desire to serve my Church; on the other hand a certain voice was calling me to—what? Something more? I didn't know.

During the four years of our study at St. Joseph's, the tension would slowly strain within me. I continued in my resolve to learn obedience, absorbing the teachings and rules of the Church, trying hard to mold myself into a pliable, acquiescent seminarian.

An influx of new students swelled our ranks and crowded the dormitory, so that a few of us were asked if we would like to sleep inside the church. I quickly volunteered, as did Faraj. Ironically, I was then able to carry on all the late-night meditations I wanted with impunity.

In 1955, the Zionist forces invaded Gaza, and a year later the Sinai, that huge, wedge-like peninsula between the new state and Egypt. With the Sinai takeover, the United States intervened, insisting that Israel withdraw to the 1948 armistice lines. Though Prime Minister Ben Gurion and his defense ministry conceded, they insisted that the invasion was necessary because Israel needed a buffer zone between itself and Egypt, whose new President Nasser was talking of uniting the Arab nations to "liberate" Palestine. The Israeli press was flooded with outcries against Arab aggression which reverberated around the world. The question of Palestinian refugees—both in and out of Israel—was obscured by sympathy for the "beleaguered" young nation.

At St. Joseph's, we watched the conflict escalate and subside, discussing the political implications with the intensity of opinionated young men. When the fighting ceased with Israeli withdrawal, some of the students expressed a relief that it was done with, and moreover, that the war had been fought in the south. Though we had experienced some tightening of the "emergency laws," the trouble had not touched us or our families this time. To a few of them, personal safety was all that mattered.

Such thinking bothered me greatly.

Were we really safe just because we were gathered under the protecting wings of the institutional Church? Or were we being lulled to sleep by our own personal security? Why were we not angry—or at least pained—at the suffering of our people in the hills and refugee camps?

All of this added to my continued inner conflicts. I wished I could remain serene—aloof and undisturbed by worldly conflicts as was Father, as were Faraj and the brothers of St. Joseph's. It did not occur to me then that my unquiet heart was not a bad thing. It was like a delicate balance that had been forcefully tipped and wanted righting. It produced in me a drive—like a hunger—that would carry me to the fiery heart of our land's vast conflict.

As my final two years in Nazareth passed, one conviction flickered dimly and grew: being a servant of God meant more than drifting above earth's struggles in an other-worldly realm like some pale figure in an icon. In this, I found encouragement from an unexpected source.

Father Ghazal was a stricter teacher than most at St.

Joseph's. His voice could sharpen to a metal edge when you gave the wrong answer, making him sound more like a career man in the military than a priest. Most of the students feared him. Somehow, beneath his bristly exterior, I thought I could detect a wonderfully sensitive heart, a true concern for our spiritual and intellectual progress.

I was seated in his lecture one day toward the end of 1957, when another student posed a question: How could one be a good Christian if, well—if certain people bothered you? If, he stammered hastily, you often got angry or impatient?

For a moment Father Ghazal was absolutely frozen, staring off into space in search of the right words.

Then he replied simply, "It's not enough to try to be good—to try to be some sort of 'saint.' You must let God occupy your body. You must be tamed by Him. He may put you through many hard things—and it is these struggles that will tame you. Then you will be ready to do His good pleasure."

How, I do not know, but I suddenly recalled the prayer I had uttered years before, just after we were exiled to Gish. Then I had asked God to use my hands and feet as His own. And now Father Ghazal was saying that a servant of God is never asked to do more than that—or less.

I smiled, wondering if it were really possible that God had taken me up on my childlike prayer, guiding me first into the care of the Bishop and then here to St. Joseph's. And more than that, I wondered if God had allowed me to feel His own heart's concern for the Palestinian people. But whenever I thought about the war, the bombing or my beating, some awful twisting thing burned inside of me—something that had yet to be tamed.

Despite the feeling, I had a flicker of conviction: I was to study, not just for ordination in the Church, but as a messenger to my people. Even so, I was amused at the thought.

What was my message? That everyone should leave their villages and become contemplatives in cloisters?

I glanced across the room at Faraj. His brows were knit in intense thought. I wished I could read his expression and know his response to Father Ghazal's comments. Since we were nearing the end of our schooling in Nazareth, we would both be expected to declare our intentions formally. Would he feel as I did?

Our entire last year was one in which I pondered my direction. A tingle of indignation burned inside me each time I heard of another tightening of the "emergency laws" that governed Palestinians in Israel—each time another village had its farm land confiscated for a *kibbutz*. At the edge of my thoughts, I wondered how I could deliver a message of heavenly peace to people—Jew or Palestinian—when they lived daily with war.

One evening in the spring of 1958, as we moved into our final semester at St. Joseph's, Faraj and I were alone in our church quarters, studying for a test. I sensed him watching me and looked up from my page.

Faraj shut his book abruptly and a sheaf of paper fluttered to the floor. He sat up and braced his long, willowy arms across his chest. We were both nearly nineteen, and while I had continued to thicken at the chest and shoulders, he had stayed slender as he grew. He stretched out his lean legs, and I retrieved his paper from the floor. Curious, I asked, "What is it? What are you thinking?"

"Elias," he began, "we've grown up just like brothers. Do you know we've been together for almost six years? And it won't be long until St. Joseph's is through with us."

"That's true. And . . . ?" I smiled, wondering what my alter-ego was getting at. He lay back on his mattress, hands braced behind his head. Suddenly he unfolded a vision of the future—our future.

"You know the Bishop is making inquiries at the seminary in Jerusalem. If things work out, we can go there together. Won't that be great? We can go together as brothers, Elias. We are brothers, aren't we?"

My heart leaped at his words: "seminary . . . together. . . ."

He went on. "And after seminary—after we're ordained—we can have a church together maybe. I've been thinking of the things Father Ghazal said about letting God occupy your body. That's what we can do. We can live simply, sharing all things in common, fifty-fifty, just like the early Christians. We can live peacefully among the poor. We can give our lives to serving them. . . ."

He talked on for some time, building a bright dream. It touched my deepest wound—the need for a home, a sense of *place*. It sounded so comforting, so easy. When he finished, I found myself agreeing to his plan, eagerly trying to fill my emptiness with someone else's dream. And in that moment, I shoved aside the unsettling thoughts and the challenging voice that beckoned me.

Daily we talked with increasing excitement about the vows we would take to live lives of charity, humility, obedience, extending God's hand of love through the villages of Galilee. We would live, I thought, as Father did, in poorness of spirit, holding everything we had in open hands before God.

However, our dream flickered once, chilled by a harsh breath of reality.

During our last weeks at St. Joseph's, while we struggled under the pressure of final examinations, the Bishop delivered one more bit of hard-hitting news. Holding back tears of pain and anger, his eyes welled as he told us evenly, "You cannot go to Jerusalem. The authorities will not allow you to cross the border to the seminary."

The seminary, a very old, Melkite school, lay outside the

borders of Israel in the part of Jerusalem apportioned by the
United Nations to the kingdom of Jordan. The Jordanians,
the Bishop explained, did not want "contaminated Palestinians from occupied territories" coming to study in their
sector of the city. Although it was the closest seminary, and
though our expressed intent was to serve the Church, the
Bishop had no power to sway the authorities. We were barred
from entering Jordan's territory. And once again our people
had been maligned with a variation of that hideous phrase,
"dirty Palestinians." How I hated that!

The Bishop, in his resourcefulness, was not about to let
this snag tear his net, allowing two live seminarians to get
away. He quickly made inquiries through his connections in
the Church hierarchy, and in a week he announced, "Elias.
Faraj. You will go to study at Saint Sulpice. A good school, a
very good school—in Paris. I've made all the arrangements."

In Paris? We were stunned. Neither of us had been outside
of Galilee, except for our sheltered schooling in Haifa, let
alone to far-off hinterlands such as Europe. But the Bishop
had decided. That was that.

When I returned to Gish after graduation, the reaction of
my family was as mixed as my own. Mother and Father were
delighted that one of their sons would study for ordination.
But in Paris? In their thinking, no one ever went to Europe
and returned. As all my remaining relatives gathered to see
me off, I saw the sadness behind their smiles.

When it was time to leave, Wardi and my brothers hugged
me one by one. Mother and Father clutched me close to them
one last time, and then released me—as parents have always
set their children free in the world—with a mixture of happiness and heartache. And now I had a sense—comforting
and challenging at the same time—that my way was narrow-
ing before me.

A week later, Faraj and I tried to get our sealegs on the rolling deck of the ship that carried us away from the port at Haifa. We stood side by side like two brothers, tall, eager and still quite sheltered about things of the world. The Bishop had given us a little money—the equivalent of ten dollars—to get us from our European port of entry in Naples, Italy, to Rome. There, he had assured us, one of his contacts would be waiting to help us. Holding onto the rail for balance, we stared in silence as the green shoreline of our land faded and was gone.

"More than six years, Elias," Faraj's voice broke the concentration. "That's a long time to be away."

I felt a tightening in my throat and could not answer. Once again the raging conflict that was Israel had driven my family apart.

I could not guess the pressures that would slowly grind and pulverize our already crippled villages. In my heart was the shining plan to return and live simply, quietly among my people, dispensing the charities of the Church. I had no thought that my life was about to take another sharp turn—that my dream of a peaceful life in service with Faraj would never be. An astonishing awakening lay ahead of me.

When we left the deck, our mood lightened a bit. And then our conversation turned to Paris.

# 7

# *The Outcasts*

No doubt Faraj and I looked like two wide-eyed boys roaming through Paris. The Seminary of St. Sulpice, a time-honored whetstone for sharpening the Church's young men, lay in one of the oldest sections of the city. Nearby was the vast Louvre Museum, the River Seine, Notre Dame, the acclaimed Sorbonne University and the opulent Luxembourg Gardens. Art galleries and expensive boutiques abounded. Even our quarters in the Italianate buildings of the seminary—perhaps humble by other standards—made us feel like kings. It was a breath-taking world of glamour, art, intellectualism, romance and prosperity beyond anything we had imagined.

One of our biggest problems was apparent at once: we spoke little French. The smatterings we had learned from the housemothers in the orphanage in Haifa was hardly enough to help when, on our first day of classes, we were sent to the Sorbonne for a lecture on the existential philosophies of Sartre. As the tweedy, chain-smoking professor embarked on a gamboling survey of Sartre, the other students looked intent, nodding their heads at appropriate moments—and

Faraj and I were bewildered. All that we could determine of the lecture was that it was not given in our language.

We faced an immediate struggle with learning to speak French. And yet, as we learned the language, we gradually detected another, more serious problem.

Among the members of the Church of St. Sulpice we found several warm friendships. A kind professor named Father Longère quickly became a confidant and a mentor for us as we tried to learn western ways. And a Miss Deville, a saintly, single woman in her middle years, often invited us for home-cooked meals. A devout Christian, she always opened her heart whenever our homesickness became unbearable. From the outset, however, we detected a certain wall between us. If ever we spoke about the troubles of our people, she would quickly turn the conversation to more genteel, less troubling matters.

Likewise, many of the other students in the seminary were friendly and often curious about our life in the "Holy Land." Of course, we never passed up a chance to talk about our home and the questions inevitably led to the 1948 war. Then a strange silence fell as we told about the displacement of nearly one million Palestinians, the deaths, the destruction of Biram and the terror that had come upon our families. Furtive glances passed from student to student, and they nodded faintly as if they were merely humoring us.

Their awkward silence was finally broken during a conversation some months after our arrival. Our French was improving rapidly, and talk had led me to recount the forced removal of the men of Biram. Faraj commented that the same fate had befallen many other villages.

"Well I suppose," said one student, nervously clearing his throat, "that the Zionists had to do something to protect themselves from terrorists."

"But we just wanted to live in peace with them," I blurted,

"to farm our land and be left alone." I could feel my cheeks coloring.

"Let's be completely honest," he plunged ahead with the air of an inquisitor. "We've heard all the news reports about Arab terrorism. The Zionists knew they had to clean out those villages or there would be no peace."

It was true that by that time, in the late 1950s, some crudely armed groups of men called the *fedayeen,* had begun to gather in the countries surrounding Israel, plotting reprisals. They were not even wanted by the countries they inhabited. But at the time our villages were sacked, no such organized groups had existed.

"Is that your idea of 'peace'?" I demanded. "That a group of foreigners should forcefully crush a whole country full of powerless people and take over their land?" I was alarmed at the force of the words that suddenly boiled out of me, as if from some long-capped well of angry frustration.

"Elias—" Faraj gripped my arm and gave a cautioning look, hoping to ease the tension. I took a deep breath, knowing it was useless to argue. Still, I could not let it go.

"Look," I said more calmly, "all Palestinians are not fighters. Nor are we the terrorists. We have been the *terrorized.* In French history your people rebelled against oppression. They became known as heroes just because they won. Had they lost, they would have been called rebels and traitors.

"Besides, you've known us for a few months," I pursued, indicating Faraj and myself. "We're not terrorists. Neither are our families. We don't want to hurt anyone. The Jews are welcome in our country, but we don't want their military to take over our farmland and our homes. Would you? We just want to bring peace back to our people. To reconcile Palestinians and Jews."

Our friend replied, "That is because you are *good* Palestinians."

We were deeply dismayed. Faraj and I were good Palestinians. Implied was the converse: most of the other Palestinian people were bad. I could not help recalling the villagers of Biram crowded into the church each Sunday, thankful for their simple life. Where had such an attitude come from? Did others feel the same way about Palestinian people?

Unfortunately, we were to learn that Palestinians, indeed, had been branded as ignorant, hostile and violent. And now, with no flag, no honor and no voice to shout our defense to the opinion-fashioning world press, the reputation of our ancient people had degenerated to the status of non-persons. We were the outcasts.

Never was this painful position more sharply apparent to me than during our first Christmas in France.

A wealthy and influential man in the church invited me to celebrate Christmas with his family and a few other guests in their country home outside Paris. Faraj had been invited by another family and so I accepted, not wanting to sit alone in the dormitory.

On Christmas Eve I was picked up outside my room and driven through the lightly falling snow to the outskirts of the city. As we drove, I fended off memories of Mother and Father, so far away. I would try to enjoy this Christmas with a substitute family.

Their manor-like home was decorated simply with elegant tapers in wall sconces warming the gloom of the winter night. I watched my hostess light the last taper when the door chimes sounded. As she whisked off to answer it, my host turned to me with an inscrutable look and said, "I plan to introduce you as our special guest. I—I hope you won't mind."

I felt flattered. I couldn't imagine why I should mind and merely nodded.

The children were passing a tray of steaming cider with

cinnamon, and our hostess had disappeared with the coats. As a newly-arrived couple entered the room, my host introduced me, "This is Elias Chacour."

I extended my hand. "Pleased to meet you. I am from the village of Bi—"

"From *Bethlehem!*" my host interrupted, clapping me on the back. "Elias is a Jewish student at our seminary. Can you imagine? I thought it would be a lovely surprise to have a Jewish believer from the holy land to celebrate Christmas with us," he finished with a jaunty smile.

The visitors were delighted. I stared at him in disbelief. Why was he lying about me? At my first opportunity, before any more guests arrived, I pulled him aside to ask if he had made some mistake.

"Tonight you are *Jewish—from Bethlehem,"* he said with a cool smile. "That's not such a big favor to ask, is it? You'll get along much better if you stop announcing to the world that you are Palestinian."

I was crushed. His main reason for inviting me to his home had not been kindness, but to display me as a Christmas Eve attraction. For the rest of the evening, he continued to introduce me as a young Jewish man from Bethlehem. I was too embarrassed to contradict him—and I felt miserable.

After this incident, Faraj and I became increasingly aware that, in western eyes, being Palestinian was a disgraceful thing—a stigma like leprosy. And as we entered the decade of the 1960s, that wounded reputation would be dealt a vicious blow. More bands of the *fedayeen* gathered at Israel's borders like a tightening noose.

During those first few years at seminary, I felt another tension between the simple spirituality I had inherited through generations and the modern Church philosophies. In my second and third years in Paris, I was increasingly concerned that all of our instruction was in subjects like Church dogma, rituals, rites and rules. Though my grades were high and I had a quick facility for learning both ancient and modern languages, I was ever uneasy. Where was the deep spiritual wisdom, the strength I had hoped to find? When it came to theology classes, I always seemed to upset the professors who were infected by the newly-popular philosophies of the day.

One professor in logics particularly delighted in taking blade-like slashes at my work. During his class, we were assigned to write a paper on the "proper view of God in the atomic age." The topic amused me a little: to think that God needed to be "properly viewed" by seminarians as if He were a minute germ under a microscope. I wondered if, in preparing to serve God, we ought not to consider how He might be viewing us.

Nevertheless, I carefully fashioned my argument, starting with the point that God had not changed from one age to another, He was "the same yesterday, today and forever" as the New Testament proclaimed. He was ever-present with us, not "dead" as modern philosophy declared. I finished with the strong assertion that we were the ones who removed ourselves from God's love by our hateful, violent actions toward each other.

A week later the paper was returned with a failing grade emblazoned across the top in red ink. Beneath it, the professor had scrawled angry comments that began, "This is not logic, but *illogic*." In his scathing denunciation, he said that reasoning from a scriptural viewpoint was not acceptable. I should have begun with the problem of man, the primate, lost in an endless search for the "God idea." To this poor professor God was absent and men were hopelessly alienated. Unfortunately, he was not the only one of this persuasion who was teaching us seminarians.

That afternoon, Faraj and I strolled along the Seine. I had to get away from the seminary after such a blasting. First, we visited the Cathedral of Notre Dame, seeking a quiet place. But today the very splendor of the structure, which usually comforted me, was disturbing. I stared at the glorious rose window, afire with sunlight, and all I could think of was the simple church in Biram that we had also called Notre Dame. It had nourished my spirit. Now it was half rubble.

Leaving the cathedral, we sauntered past a sidewalk artist dabbing at bright, blue-green tempera impressions of the river, and Faraj brought me back to my troubles in logics class. "I thought your paper was excellent, Elias," he said trying to cheer me. "He was too brutal. I don't understand it."

"There is something *else* I don't understand. People have so much here—nice homes, cars, clothes—and so little faith. Both Catholic and Protestant churches are almost empty. What's happened here?"

Faraj nodded. "People in the West seem so taken with material things. It's as if they have nothing in their spirits, so they need to surround themselves with nice comforts." He paused and leaned against a rail at the river's edge. "I hate to say it, but that sort of thinking seems to have invaded the Church, too.

"The real problem," he said after a moment's silence, "is that Western theology starts with man as the center of all things and tries to force God into some scheme that we can understand. Then He can be regulated. Elias, we've grown up believing that God is the beginning and end of all things. He is central, not an afterthought. He's alive and has His own ways. Here, they want to tame God with their philosophy."

"Worse than that," I countered. "I'm afraid the Western philosophies have *killed* God. If there's no respect for Him, what value do men have? Without God there is no compassion, no humanity."

As we crossed a bridge heading for the Boulevard St. Germain and the seminary, I voiced the doubts that had been nagging me for weeks: "Why are we studying here? What is seminary really preparing us for?"

Swiftly, Faraj corrected me. "We've come to be trained to serve our Church. Don't forget that."

We walked on quietly together. And though we hardly noticed then, his words had fallen like a faint shadow between us, a first small parting. Even as we continued to train for ordination, I was being prepared for a riskier calling than he or I knew.

To me, it is an eternal irony that two young men whose dream was to shun the world, to live in peace and simplicity, should land themselves in Europe in the 1960s. Vast upheavals were overturning the Western culture. Life seemed a confusion of questions.

Politically it was the fear-filled era of the Cold War. Nations that were supposedly Christian and moral could justify violence by pointing to the end result. In the name of establishing democracy, any horror might be employed at the expense of humanity itself. As the world moved through the Cold War and beyond, how many rulers would be deposed or killed with the secret help of Western democracies? How many innocents would be tortured or seared with napalm by the "peacekeeping" forces of the powerful nations? Had contact with the West infected the Zionists, deadening the ancient voices of their prophets? And from the Church, no voice was heard. Those who wanted to catapult it out of its medieval slumber and into the twentieth century, were resisted by conservatives, fearful of losing long-held power and position.

Little wonder that my head was befogged: My self-worth was at its lowest ebb, the entire world was being threatened by the "Bomb" and the Church to which I was giving my life was in upheaval. How deeply I understood the spring-loaded tension of those Palestinian *fedayeen* as the world went blind to our plight in the Middle East.

Then in 1962, a strange event took place that would leave its mark on me forever after.

I was traveling by train to visit some new-found friends in West Germany. The train glided through the rolling green hills of eastern France, skirting some luscious and very old vineyards which sent my thoughts across the miles to the land that had once been ours in Israel.

A conductor sauntered down the swaying aisle. "West German border in five minutes," he announced. "Have your passports ready, please."

I fished in my travel bag for my identification papers, but my mind was on the jumble of events in the recent past and the tragic news.

A letter from Israel had arrived several months before and I had torn into it with my usual eagerness. It was not a light, newsy letter, but one that deeply cut my heart. My brother, Chacour, was dead.

Chacour, who had married during my years in Haifa, had been laboring hard at a construction job in the Carmel mountain range when he suffered something like a stroke. For almost forty days he had struggled for his life in a hospital before his heart gave out in the exertion. Now his young wife was left with eight small children.

As tragic as the news was, I felt even worse that I had no money with which to travel home to console his wife. However, I was granted some time off from my studies to seek some quiet at a Christian retreat. I was sitting alone on a bench in a gloom of private thought, when a beautiful, small, blond child with eyes the color of the sky toddled by and smiled up into my face. We struck up an immediate friendship, perhaps because the rudimentary German I had learned recently was as infant-like as his. Wolfgang was his name, and before I knew it, he had scrambled onto my lap, giggling. Soon I, too, was chuckling.

When his parents found him, we also became instant friends. Franz and Lony Gruber were an amazingly tenderhearted couple who shared my grief at once when I told them about Chacour's death. Almost unbelievably, it was as if we were true family to each other. Generously, they insisted I visit them at their home in West Germany. It was to be the first of many, many visits that would bind us together.

The hiss and squeal of the train's brakes brought me back to the present. We had pulled up to a railway siding in a border town that was picture-postcard lovely. A white-sided town hall, with its precisely regulated clock, rose against blue, snowpeaked mountains. On the platform I could see the dark-suited officials walking toward the cars to inspect our passports which the attendant had taken from us.

Then the phenomenal thing happened.

It was as if I were flung back through time twenty-five years. With uncanny clarity, I felt as if I were crossing into Germany in 1937, and in my imagination the scene had changed vividly. Men in dark green helmets and high black boots stood with their machine guns slung over their shoulders. On their woolen uniforms glowered the red and black swastikas of the Third Reich. They were demanding our papers, looking for—what? Here and there they pulled a passport from the pile, ordering its Jewish owner to step off the train. And I with an Israeli passport! Would they call for me? Men and women were stepping fearfully from their coaches, hugging small children, huddling together miserably. They would be taken to other destinations—never to be seen again.

A trickle of sweat slipped down my temple, rousing me from the mental image. My heart beat rapidly. I was handed my passport and we continued our trip into West Germany. But the impression was burned into me as if by a brand.

Lony and Franz met me at the station, smiling brightly, over-joyed to see me. And I them. We were, indeed, to become as family before I left Europe. But throughout that visit, the strange image would haunt me.

For the first time that twisting dark feeling inside me was matched—if not totally overruled—by another feeling: the ache of compassion. It was as if some calming hand was beginning to tame a wild creature within me. I hurt for the Jewish people. Why had the civilized world allowed them to be persecuted?

Other questions were just as troubling. Why did the world allow my people to be driven into diaspora only a few years after the Holocaust? Surely the Jews knew the horror of militarism—why had they used such violence against my people? How had the minds of the nations been poisoned to think of Palestinians as an idle, worthless people capable of nothing but violence?

These questions drove me, and soon I would be startled as I discovered the treachery that brought disaster to my people—the political power plays that set the Middle East ablaze with turmoil.

# 8

# *Seeds of Hope*

Upon my return to Paris I was haunted by the mystery that had opened itself to me on the train into West Germany: What was the true story of Palestine? I was aware as never before that people in the West held a view that went something like this. The Jewish people, having suffered tremendous persecution, needed a haven—a national homeland. Their Zionist leaders had chosen the "uninhabited" land of Palestine. Supposedly, the surrounding Arab nations were naturally antagonistic and jealous that the Jewish settlers had turned a wasteland into a paradise. They had risen unprovoked against the Jews, forcing them to fight a valiant War of Independence in 1948.

But I had grown up in Palestine in those years and that was not the full story, nor was it especially correct. I had witnessed a terribly ironic twist of history in which the persecuted became the persecutor. As one of its victims, I had seen the cruel face of Zionism.

Now I determined to find out how a peaceful movement that had begun with a seemingly good purpose—to end the persecution of the Jewish people—had become such a destructive, oppressive force.

Along with that determination, I was driven by a respect for history that Father had planted in me. Did the seeds of our future hope lie buried in our past, as he had so often said?

Aside from my seminary studies I began to spend hours in the libraries of Paris, hunting down books and news reports on the true history of the Zionists and the Palestine disaster. Whole books and reports unifying these accounts would not be published until years later. Yet my study pieced together a startling, documented story.

In 1897, I learned, a conference had convened in Basle, Switzerland, to "lay the foundation stone of the house which was to shelter the Jewish nation." The director of the gathering was a prominent writer named Theodor Herzl. He had fathered in Europe a new political movement called Zionism—an inspiring movement that hoped to rescue the downtrodden, impoverished and humiliated Jews in the big city ghettoes. By the end of the conference the delegates had agreed on two points—a flag and an anthem, the symbols of their unity and purpose. Beyond the pomp and emotional fervor the delegates were split on the location of this homeland that was being pushed by the leadership: Palestine.

Immediately, many disputed Herzl's statement that Palestine was a "land without a people, waiting for a people without a land." Though Herzl had been willing to contemplate settlement in Argentina or Uganda as alternatives, his sights were clearly set on the Middle East. It was to this proposal that many delegates primarily and strenuously objected. By what right could Zionists expect to create a state in Palestine? It was a land with established borders and, more importantly, it had long been *inhabited* by people of an ancient, respectable culture. A homeland in Palestine, they declared with the overtones of a heinous prophecy, would have to be forgotten—or else established by force.

Devout Jews within and without the movement—particularly the Orthodox—fervently argued that Zionism was a blasphemy, because the elite, non-religious Jews felt that Zionism was the only Messiah Israel would ever have. Such talk incensed the religious, as did the hints of militarism that already colored the fringes of the movement. Others, less religious and more pragmatic, believed that Zionism would feed anti-Semitism since it underscored the long-criticized, "exclusiveness" of the Jewish people. They saw clearly that no land could be simply, peacefully "resettled" without violence.

Therefore, to appease the religious consciences the Zionist leaders adopted the principles of non-violence embodied in the Jewish *Havlaga*. This helped to rally the support of the masses, the multiple millions who desperately hoped for an escape from the growing pogroms against them in Europe. Yet the leaders continued to formulate designs on Palestine. Though Herzl would not live much beyond the turn of the century, others would push his plans forward.

In Palestine, my own people were under too tight a thumb to take much notice of a conference in Basle, even if they had known of it. In the early 1900s, ours was also a downtrodden people, struggling and praying for freedom from our own oppressors. For hundreds of years we had suffered under the iron heel of the Turkish Ottoman Empire. When World War I engulfed the Middle East, the empire had already begun to totter.

After the war, as the empire crumbled, the Palestinian people felt the first winds of freedom. The League of Nations bore their hopes aloft further by proposing a plan that would help "subject peoples." Larger, powerful nations would assist weaker nations in establishing their own independent governments. This was known as the Mandate system.

The British, who desired a foothold of power in the Middle East, saw in the Mandate system a great opportunity. Secretly, they made a proposal to Palestinian leaders: The British would help oust the Turks; in return, they would set up a temporary Mandate government in Palestine with the promise that they would slowly withdraw, leaving an established, independent country governed by the Palestinians themselves. In desperation, the Palestinian leaders agreed to this strategy. Freedom was in sight—or so they supposed—and little notice was given to the tiny Jewish agricultural communities that were sprouting in a seemingly scattered fashion across the landscape.

What I learned next in my readings truly saddened me. Once the British rule was established, the story became convoluted with political intrigues and double-dealings.

Immediately, the British met in secret with the French and Russians to divide the Middle East into "spheres of influence" with Palestine to be governed, not by the people of Palestine as promised, but by an international administration. The secret agreement was uncovered several years later, in 1917, when the Bolsheviks overthrew the czarist regime and could not resist making public such "imperialist" duplicity. Palestinian leaders were dismayed at this news and at once sent delegates to the British to protest. They chose the diplomatic route while an elite group, whose sights were set on Palestine, had already begun influencing British bureaucrats.

The year 1917 will forever be scarred with the brand of infamy for the Palestinian people. The Zionists had aligned themselves with Great Britain's Christian Restorationists, a group that believed they might bring to pass—by manipulating world events and reestablishing the nation of Israel—the Second Coming of Christ. The Zionists ignored this view, but the benefits of such a plan for them were obvious. They saw in Britain's new hold on Palestine their secret inroad to the Middle East, and so began a strange marriage between Zion-

ist and Restorationist. It was in 1917 that the British Lord
Arthur Balfour made his famous declaration—not in public
at first, but privately in a letter to the powerful Lord Roth-
schild.

Lord Balfour wrote that the Cabinet "viewed with favor
the establishment of a national home for the Jewish people"
in Palestine. And in the same letter, with a stroke of the pen,
he reclassified the people of Palestine—ninety-two percent
of the population—as "non-Jewish communities."[3] Not only
did this renege on the promise of independence, but it effectively handed over Palestine to the Zionists. The prime
mover behind the British decision was the Zionist leader,
Chaim Weizmann.

If Lord Balfour was acting out of his own religious conviction or a love for the Jewish people, as some historians
declared, I was unconvinced. In 1906, he had played a major
part in passing the Aliens Act which expressly sought to
exclude Jews from Great Britain. Nor was Lord Balfour
oblivious of the political treachery in which he was enweb-
bed. In 1919, in a memorandum to the British Cabinet, he
declared:

> In Palestine we do not propose even to go
> through the form of consulting the wishes of the
> present inhabitants of the country. So far as Pal-
> estine is concerned, (we) have made no statement
> of fact which is not admittedly wrong, and no decla-
> ration of policy which at least in the letter (we) have
> not always intended to violate. [4]

To me, it seemed that the Zionists had entered into an
unholy marriage, an alliance motivated by power and convenience, consummated in treachery.

At once, Palestinian leaders were dismayed. For the next
sixteen years they continually presented their fears to the

British through diplomatic channels, appealing continually to royal commissions while unrest grew throughout Palestine. And the Zionists, funded by international money collected by the Jewish Agency, rapidly settled *kibbutzim* in a clearer and clearer pattern throughout Palestine, slowly forming the skeletal outlines of the land they meant to declare as their own homeland.

Through the 1920s, European immigration to Palestine rose dramatically and the Zionist leaders became less and less guarded about their plan. Weizmann told an American secretary of state that he hoped "Palestine would ultimately become as Jewish as England is English." [5] And thereafter, another Zionist leader told British officials, "There can only be one National Home in Palestine, and that a Jewish one, and no equality in the partnership between Jews and Arabs, but a Jewish predominance as soon as the numbers of that race are sufficiently increased." [6]

Increasingly, many Zionists themselves were ill at ease with those who insisted on Jewish "predominance" in Palestine. Yitzhak Epstein, an agriculturist, had warned an international congress of the Zionist Party that they had wrongly consulted every political power that held sway over Palestine without consulting the Palestinians themselves. He feared the fact that Palestinian peasants had already lost so much land as a result of Zionist purchases from absentee landlords, and that this loss was sure to breed resentment. He argued that since the incoming Jews were bringing with them a higher standard of living, they ought to help the Palestinians to find their own identity, to open to them the new Jewish hospitals, schools and reading rooms that were already in existence or in planning stages. And when institutions for higher education were established, the Jews could strengthen their old fraternal bonds with surrounding Arab nations by opening these schools to their students as well.

Unfortunately, Epstein was staunchly opposed. His detractors shouted, "To give—always to give, to the one our body, to the other, our soul, and to yet another the remnant of the hope ever to live as a free people in its historical homeland!"[7]

And though Epstein's vision of unity between Arab and Jew was overlooked by the Zionist main body, others would take up his cause until Zionism itself was riddled with factions. At the end of the 1920s, a group calling themselves *Brit Shalom* split from the Party, because they could no longer go along with the tactic of disenfranchising the Palestinians from their land in order to set up a Jewish homeland. Sadly, this group was also largely ignored. I mentally underscored these crucial details, important clues from history that could not be overlooked. All Jews did not hate Palestinians. In fact, many recognized our brotherhood and had come to Palestine with hands extended in friendship. Were there any in the 1960s who wanted reconciliation and not war? Was this fact, somehow, one of the seeds of hope?

By the 1930s, with the influx of European settlers rising like a floodtide, with no intervention by the British, and with the plan to displace the Palestinian people in motion, what were their leaders to do? Diplomatically, they might as well have been mute. No one was listening. In 1935, in port cities like Jaffa, anti-immigration demonstrations erupted into violence and bloodshed in which both Jewish immigrants and Palestinian peasants died.

As I read about these demonstrations in the context of history, I was moved anew by the frustration the leaders of Palestine must have suffered. As a Christian I could not condone the bloodshed—but it was suddenly, sharply clear that their tension had built for almost twenty years before it reached the point of explosion. The demonstrations were an extreme measure born out of a desperation to be heard.

The following year, 1936, Palestinian leaders again tried a

peaceful means of protest, calling for a general strike. Throughout Palestine, office and factory workers, taxi and truck drivers disappeared from their jobs for a full six months, crippling commerce. But violence, which had already crept into the conflict, increased. The powerful *Histraduth* trade union, established by the Zionists and led by David Ben Gurion, terrorized Jewish shop and factory owners who dared to employ Palestinians. Here and there, Jewish women were attacked in the market places for buying from Palestinian merchants. Palestinian fields and vineyards were vandalized. Orchards were guarded to keep out all but Jewish workers. At the end of 1938, the protests were finally crushed.

By that time the Zionists had behind them an overwhelming swell of world sympathy. This was true for two main reasons: First, Western nations were little concerned with events in the Middle East because they were fixated on the horror that was spreading from Nazi Germany; second, they were appalled at the insane hatred for the Jewish people propagated by Adolph Hitler. Rightly, the Jews needed somewhere to escape from this madman.

But if Western consciences were troubled, it did not translate into action. Throughout the 1930s, while Hitler's pogroms thrived, no major western nation increased its quota of Jewish immigrants. Was the tiny land of Palestine really expected to absorb millions of European Jews, its inhabitants giving up land and jobs while the large western nations were comfortably silent?

To me, these terrified masses of Jewish immigrants were never to blame for our tragedy. They were dazed by fear, pathetically desperate to escape the heinous death camps. In this, they were to become the pawns of the Zionist leaders. Upon their arrival in Palestine they were quickly indoctrinated against their so-called new enemy—the Palestinians.

Here was the second bastion of Zionist power: propaganda. Increasingly, they controlled all news emanating from Palestine. With the tongues of our leaders effectively "cut out," it was easy to mold Western opinion through the press, obscuring the real issues. The protests of 1936-38 were renamed "The Arab Rebellion." Palestinians, who in any other country being overtaken by a foreign force would have been called freedom fighters, were "terrorists" and "guerillas." Hence, the widely used term, "Palestinian terrorist" was ingrained in the Western mind.

Proof of the Zionist power hold in Palestine came in 1939. Suffering some belated pangs of conscience, Britain issued its "White Paper," instructing its Mandate government to bar further land purchases and immigration. Immediately, the Zionists decried this move as a betrayal. Unfortunately for the British, they had effectively trained a strong Zionist underground—the *Haganah*—in special brands of violence that were now turned against British soldiers and government workers in Palestine. British General Wingate had trained the *Haganah* in the use of large, destructive barrel-bombs and how to force Palestinian men to "confess" by shoving fistfuls of sand down their throats. Should it have surprised the British when the *Irgun*, bombed the King David Hotel killing almost one hundred people?

World War II forced a lull in the struggle for Palestine. But for Zionist leaders, the outcome was never in question.

Following the war the Zionists shifted their power push from Downing Street to the White House. Primarily, the British, who had now shown themselves reluctant to impose a Jewish state on Palestine, had been severely weakened. It was unwieldy and expensive to continue governing Palestine, and the Zionists had gained all but total control of munitions factories and industries there. More importantly, the U.S. had emerged as the new leader in determining the future of the free world. And in America a strong lobby of new Zionist supporters had emerged. What happened then, in the closed conference rooms of the White House, was no less scandalous than the British betrayal.

While President Roosevelt was in office he had resisted the pressure of Zionists, unwilling to see the Palestinians displaced from their homeland. He felt tremendous compassion for the half-million survivors who were expected to emerge from the Holocaust, but he had in mind a wonderfully humanitarian plan. He intended to open the free world to these pitiable victims, offering them passage to any free nation that rallied to his relief effort. However, when his emissary Morris Ernst was sent to sound out international opinion, Ernst was shocked to hear himself "decried, sneered at and attacked" as a traitor by Zionists who by then had raised $46 million to lobby for their own plan.[8]

When Truman took office after Roosevelt's untimely death, the lobbyists had a fresh opportunity, pressuring the new president. They argued vehemently that admission to Palestine was "the only hope of survival" for the Jewish people. Could this have been true when millions of Jewish people had been sheltered and protected by free nations during the war? When in fact, Jewish people throughout the free world moved easily in their societies, enjoying high standards of living in Western countries without discrimination? Nevertheless, when Truman was confronted by Arab leaders, the Zionist lobby had already done its job effectively. Truman's response: "I am sorry, gentlemen, but I have to answer to hundreds of thousands of those who are anxious for the success of Zionism; I do not have hundreds of thousands of Arabs among my constituents."[9]

Thus the vast majority of the Holocaust victims were never given a choice as to where they would live; only twenty thousand were admitted to large, free countries like the U.S.

in the three years following the war. Thus the exhausted British found themselves pressured by the most powerful office in the world, the White House, even as they watched their Mandate government in Palestine be blitzed by a campaign of terror. Guns, grenades, bombs and tanks—all manufactured in factories the British themselves had built—were now used against them.

In April 1947, war-weary and unwilling to lose more young men to defend Palestine from the Zionist underground, the British announced the plan to surrender their Mandate in one year. They were beaten and humiliated. Relinquishing Palestine was their only solution to the double-dealings they had begun thirty years before.

And as the British washed their hands of the Palestinian people they had promised to protect, violence spread unchecked. To the world, the Zionists proclaimed that they were fighting a "War of Independence." And the world, now penitent about the Holocaust, applauded. So the terror found its way into every village, even into the far hills of Galilee—and into my own home in Biram.

Sadly, the violence did not stop there.

In the years following the declaration of the State of Israel, its government needed desperately to flood the new land with settlers. Despite their claim that Israel was the one hope for Jewish survival, Jewish people in America were comfortable in their homes and businesses. Likewise, large Jewish communities in other countries showed no compulsion to uproot *en masse* and rush to the "promised land." Something had to be done. While the offerings of romance and adventure had some drawing effect on pioneering minds in America, another more sinister technique was used elsewhere. I learned much later that the Jewish community in Iraq, for instance, became the victim of "anti-Semitic" violence of suspicious origin.

On the last evening of Passover in April 1950, some fifty thousand Jewish people, celebrating an ancient tradition, were enjoying a stroll along the Tigris River in Baghdad. More than 130,000 Jewish people lived in Iraq, forming the oldest Jewish community in the world. Few of them had emigrated to Israel, though the way was freely open to them. Out of the darkness a car sped along the river esplanade and a small bomb was hurled, exploding on the pavement.

Though no one was hurt, shock-waves of fear rocked the Jewish community. Rumors of uncertain origin spread: A new, fanatic Arab group was planning a Jewish pogrom. It seemed unreasonable to many, since Jews had lived undisturbed in Iraq for a long time. But leaflets appeared mysteriously the very next day urging Jews to flee to Israel—and ten thousand signed up for emigration immediately. Where had the leaflets come from? How had they appeared so instantly?

The mystery was forgotten when a second bomb exploded—then a third, killing several people outside a synagogue. The rumors flew. By early 1951, Jews fled Iraq in panic, abandoning homes, property and an ancient heritage until only five thousand remained in the country.

Some fifteen people were arrested in connection with the bombing—and the remnant of the Jewish community was outraged. The *Haganah*, it was discovered, had smuggled arms caches into Iraq and it was *they* who had thrown the bombs at their own Jewish people. Their plan to touch off a panic emigration to Israel had worked. The Israeli Prime Minister David Ben Gurion and Yigal Allon, later to become Foreign Minister, knew of the plot. It was their way of helping along the prophesied "ingathering" of the Jews—even if the method was anti-biblical. If the world press was given to believe that hateful Arabs were responsible, it simply bolstered public sympathy for the "struggling" nation.

Years later, no less a reputable leader than the Chief Rabbi of Iraq, Sassoon Khedurri, pleaded with an inquiring journalist to tell the world the truth about Zionism. Not only had Jews in Iraq felt sympathy for the plight of the Palestinian people, but they too had suffered at the hands of the Zionist. Khedduri stated:

> By mid-1949 the big propaganda guns were already going off in the United States. American dollars were going to save Iraqi Jews—whether Iraqi Jews needed saving or not. There were daily "pogroms" in the *New York Times* and under datelines which few noticed were from Tel Aviv. Why didn't someone come to see *us* instead of negotiating with Israel to take in Iraqi Jews? Why didn't someone point out that the solid, responsible leadership of Iraqi Jews believed this [Iraq] to be their country? . . . The Iraqi government was being accused of holding the Jews against their will . . . campaigning among Jews was increased. . . . The government was whip-sawed . . . accused of pogroms and violent actions against Jews. . . . But if the government attempted to suppress Zionist agitation attempting to stampede the Iraqi Jews, it was again accused of discrimination.[10]

Amid the troubling facts, I thought I glimpsed more answers. I could not help but view the Zionists as victims, too—victims of something far worse than death camps. Beyond the hurling of bombs, the murder of innocents and bearing to the world false witness against their neighbor, the Zionists were stricken with a disease of the spirit. It was as if some demon of violence had been loosed and it whispered cunningly, *Might is right. Achieve your own ends by what-*

*ever means necessary—all in the name of God.* While the Church was sadly stumbling over its modern philosophies, this demon blinded the nations to the laws of the universe: Peace can never be achieved by violence; violence begets more violence. For the first time I saw clearly the face of my true enemy and the enemy of all who are friends of God and of peace. It was not the Zionists, but the demon of Militarism.

At the same time, something seethed beneath my ribs. The thought of such betrayal raised in me a feeling I had squelched so long I could hardly admit to it—much less name it. I gritted my teeth and shook off the feeling as if it were a spider that had crept onto my hand.

A more pressing question helped to obscure my feelings—the stark question of my own future. It was spring 1965, the end of my years in seminary was fast approaching, and I was just about to reach the shining ideal for which Faraj and I had come to Paris. I had set out to serve God and man in quietness and simplicity, dispensing the routine graces of the Church. For a time I had even tried to quell that outspoken nature of mine. Though I had done my best to feed my contemplative side, something like wildfire still burned through my sinews. It was as if I'd been driven to uncover this historical perspective—although Faraj had sometimes cautioned me not to be side-tracked. Had I angled onto another path—or was I slowly, truly finding the dead-center direction of my life's calling? I was a little unnerved to realize that I could not now live as that parochial priest I had once dreamed of becoming.

When, one evening, I opened my thoughts fully to Faraj, I hoped he would immediately agree with me. Late April was upon us and we were sauntering along the elegant Rue De Rivoli where trees were in full bud and the boutiques were just lighting their neon signs against the dusk. We had been as close as brothers for more than fourteen years, and Faraj's youthful charm had continued to mature into a quiet spirituality that I still admired. I hoped that he would help to sort out my conflicting thoughts.

"If I were merely railing against a political system, that would be one thing," I explained as we walked through the thinning crowds of shoppers. "Then I'd become a politician, too. But I believe it's more than that. It's a spiritual sickness. There are unholy alliances between nations that talk about God while their true motives are purely military."

"You can hardly expect to change what's happened," Faraj replied.

"But I do."

"How? You don't throw bombs," he retorted.

"Of course not," I said quickly.

"Then what? I'll tell you. You must wait patiently, Elias. God will move in His time. We must accept all things as from His hand. It's no good to try to upset a whole government. Even a repressive one."

I stared at Faraj. For an instant I saw the face of Father—the faces of the village elders of Biram. Here was that old question that had troubled me so long: As a Christian do you speak out against the actions of your enemies—or do you allow them to crush the life out of you? So many seemed to think that submitting to humiliation was the only Christian alternative. Should you not, sometimes, be stinging and preserving like salt?

Faraj was silent for a time. We had reached the Place de la Concorde where thousands of French people, including clergy, were guillotined for speaking against France's revolutionary "freedom fighters." Then he spoke firmly, "We must serve the Church quietly."

In that moment, I understood a crucial lesson: *Not all are called to the same task.* Both Faraj and I were to be ordained—but each to a special calling. He had come to feel very strongly about the wealth and extravagance of the Church amid poor and hungry people. It was for them that he hoped to help reform the Church itself. And I—I would have to find my own calling on a lonelier path that would lead away from my closest friend. In more than six years in Paris, our paths, if not our spirits, had grown apart.

For me, a door seemed to stand wide open—to *what* end I was not sure—and unmistakably I was being beckoned to step through it.

It was during our final spring days at St. Sulpice, that my kindly mentor, Father Longère, touched a deeply resonant note, like a voice out of eternity. I had come to value his wisdom, his remarkable way of challenging us, spurring us to deeper thought on any subject in which we were certain of our opinion. During one of his final lectures, I found myself riveted to his words.

"If there is a problem somewhere," he said with his dry chuckle, "this is what happens. Three people will try to do something concrete to settle the issue. Ten people will give a lecture analyzing what the three are doing. One hundred people will commend or condemn the ten for their lecture. One thousand people will argue about the problem. And *one person*—only one—will involve himself so deeply in the true solution that he is too busy to listen to any of it."

"Now," he asked gently, his penetrating eyes meeting each of ours in turn, "which person are you?"

Faraj and I were soon caught up in plans for our return trip home. I barely had time for one more trip to see Lony, Franz and Wolfgang. A letter had arrived from them in which they were insistent—politely demanding—that I not leave Europe without a final visit.

When I got to Germany, they surprised me with a "going away" gift: a brand new white Volkswagen. I was fairly speechless at their tremendous generosity. Truly our love for each other, and my love for their beautiful blond son, had grown deep. But I had never expected such kindness.

Scarcely had I learned how to handle the Volkswagen, when it was time to drive to Genoa, Italy, where a ship would carry me and my car to Haifa. As I drove to the Italian coast, I had no idea how many nights I was to think of Lony, Franz and Wolfgang, nor how unusually thankful I would be for this vehicle.

As the ship slipped from its moorings, I watched the waving crowds on the dock alone. Faraj had made other travel plans, and we would meet again in Nazareth for our ordination ceremony in July.

Now, my thoughts dwelt on seeing my family again, holding each one of them. I was bursting with eagerness.

For a brief moment, I was surprised by another feeling: I would miss Europe—miss the luxuries of the easy life. I admit the thought of remaining in Paris or Germany had tempted me at times. Having lived in a free land where I had studied, traveled and eaten in cafes without harassment, I was hardly ready to become a person without an identity again nor to face the creeping disease that sucked the spirit and hope out of my people.

# 9

## *Grafted In*

A thin wisp of smoke curled toward the high-vaulted ceiling of St. Joseph's Church—the white, sweet smoke of frankincense. Our ordination ceremony had begun. I glanced at Faraj who sat beside me at the front of the church. Was he as jittery as I? He looked as calm as ever, though I noticed that perspiration dampened his forehead.

From where we sat, I could see that the church was filled. Outside, the Mediterranean sun was white-hot. We had been back for a month and spring had turned to scorching summer. But it was the faces—the rows and rows of faces—that seemed to make us warm and moist beneath the collar, for the expansive stone church was quite cool. Almost every relative and friend I could name—those who were still in the country—had come to Nazareth for the ceremony. There were Mother and Father, seated near the front. The brothers and students of St. Joseph's school had packed the church to the doors. Though the Melkite ordination is quite unelaborate, it was a grand moment for us, culminating more than ten years of preparation. Father Longère had even traveled from Paris to celebrate with us.

Though I trembled nervously, I felt something else. What

was it? Certainly I had worked hard for this moment, had earned top grades, and along the way, learned to speak eight languages. Now the rigorous training was over. And instead of the settled feeling you find upon reaching a goal, a nagging inner voice told me that I had not yet found my true life's work.

What was more distracting were the images that kept flashing through my head while I was supposed to be concentrating on the ceremony. Two experiences since my return played through my head. . . .

I was standing at the customs line at the port in Haifa. I had just arrived from Europe, anxious to see my family. The doors to the outer waiting area opened for just a moment and in the throng I caught a glimpse of Mother and Father looking, though they were now in their early sixties, much grayer than I expected. In that moment, they smiled and pointed to the accompanying mob of family members, including Wardi, my brothers and the families that had grown around them. Then the door slammed shut.

When my turn came, I slid my passport across the counter to the customs agent. He glanced at it, then looked at me without expression. "You must go to that room over there," he said, pointing to a windowless door.

"Excuse me," I fumbled, "but why? My passport is current—"

"You are Palestinian?"

"Yes. But my family is waiting. Can't you—"

"You must go to that room. I can't stamp your passport for entry."

In the small room, I sat nervously as a brusque young man questioned me at length. For half an hour he demanded to know the names of all the places I'd been to in Europe and the names of all my "contacts." He was obviously not satisfied that I was a returning seminary student. I grew impatient with the questioning—and more than a little fearful—but I dared not become testy with him.

Finally he said in a commanding voice: "Strip."

"Excuse me?"

"*Strip*," he said more angrily. "Take off all your clothes. You must be searched."

That was my limit. "No," I said firmly. "I do not strip."

"You *will* strip or you will not get back into the country."

Moistness soaked my shirt. It was entirely likely that he could carry out his threat and not admit me. With all the calmness I could muster, I dug through my bag.

He looked at me warily. "What are you doing?"

"You are not going to admit me. And I am not going to strip for you," I replied. "And so I am going to sit here and read a book." With that I took out a book I had bought for the voyage and opened it to the first page.

Our stalemate ended after eight nerve-wracking hours. I did not strip, and was finally admitted to my home country. Outside the customs building my family swarmed around—concerned, relieved, thankful. From them I learned that travel anywhere, even by taxi, was frighteningly uncertain for all Palestinians. At any moment, you were subject to search and interrogation. . . .


The Bishop was still intoning, but another memory played in my mind.

. . . It was dusk. I had driven to a small village to visit a cousin from Biram. I was about to park in the street when he rushed out to stop me.

"Park in the yard—up near the house," he said anxiously. "It's not good to leave your car in the street here."

I was curious. Why should I be afraid to leave my car on the street in so pleasant a village?

Once inside his home I learned the reason. Most Palestinian young people were flat-handedly excluded from the universities. The reason given was that they did not have adequate education—but then, most of the village schools were poor and inferior. So even the brightest students faced lives as factory workers. And for a Palestinian girl there was little hope. As a result of such frustration, drug and alcohol abuse had slowly gone rampant and vandalism grew into an epidemic. Hence, my cousin had urged me to park my car close to the house. Our young people, the treasure of our society, could not cope with a futureless existence.

I also learned that small bands of *fedayeen* had grown and that they were striking across the borders into Israel from Lebanon, Syria and Jordan, attacking Jewish settlements. Understandably, they could never be satisfied in the ghetto-like refugee camps in which they were wasting their lives. And now, the military was cracking down on Palestinian villages with severe measures, leveling strict curfews without warning. It was no longer safe to be found in the streets after dark. . . .

I was startled by the Bishop's voice booming my name through the echoing sanctuary. Faraj and I were presented in turn to the audience, then we greeted the Bishop. He laid his hands upon us according to the ancient custom, praying for the life of God's Spirit to flood us. Then he turned each of us to the audience again, proclaiming, "He is worthy. . . . He is worthy. . . ."

In the next few weeks, as I waited to receive my first church assignment, that word would haunt me. *Worthy.* At night I would wake and see images of aimless young men—capable, bright young men—their lives wasting. Grenades would explode and I would see children—both Palestinian and Jewish—ripped apart. Angrily, I would toss in bed, seeing my own seminary-fresh face, and I would hear the voice say, *Worthy.*

Then, I would murmur into the darkness: "How? How can I ever be worthy?" I sensed the painful gap inside me that needed to be closed, opposing feelings that needed to be reconciled in me before I could ever be a real servant of God or men.

In the days following our ordination, I felt the pull—as a compass needle is drawn irresistibly—to visit the upper Galilee. Biram, I had learned, had long been abandoned by the soldiers. I had never been back since that day in 1947, but now no one would prohibit my entering the village—my true home.

Rising early one morning I left Nazareth before daybreak. The Volkswagen hummed along the highway that threaded flatly through the orchard lands of the north, then angled onto the rising dirt and gravel roads that curved up into the shadow-green, morning hills. I reached Biram just at sun-up, parking at the edge of the open area that had once been the village square. As I stepped from the car into the cool air of dawn, a sign caught my attention. In English and Hebrew it said that these "antiquities" were "preserved and protected" by the government.

The irony jarred me. Later, I learned that these "antiquities" had become a popular site visited by tourists on guided coach trips.

I passed through the square near tumbled pillars of the Roman temple and the synagogue. The light grew and filtered warmly through the olive branches. Only the chirping birds and the crunch of my steps on gravel stirred the silence. All about me the ruined stone houses were solemn, ghost-like. I climbed a crumbled wall into the dimly lit shell of the church. In the parish house, swallows sheltered in the remaining rafters. I stood frozen, dumb-struck, nearly overcome by the sense of desolation.

And yet, at the same moment I was caught unawares by a deep sense of life. From the wrecked homes, I imagined that I heard laughter, the voices of women, men deep in conversation over cups of coffee and the scent of woodsmoke. In the church, beneath the empty and teetering stone tower from which our bell had been taken, "Alleluia" was sung by children's voices again. It occurred to me then, that even bombs could never fully destroy such reverence for God and life and the land as we had felt here.

I found that I was moving swiftly down the overgrown streets to the far edge of the village, eager for the one site I had longed to see, and with each step the years peeled back. I was once again a small boy rushing home through the fig trees with some news or nonsense to share with my brothers.

Stepping from the orchard into the yard any illusion of the past was broken. The orchard itself was a ruin. For some reason it had been deserted and now grew unpruned except by the straying winds of God. The house, too, was a shambles. The roof and loft were blown away and one entire wall. Grass and weeds sprang up from the dirt floor. I could not look upon our house for very long, and I turned away with a knot in my throat.

Something in the yard stopped me. There, firmly rooted and still green with life, grew my special fig tree. I went to it and ran my hand over the rough bark and the grapevine that still trellised up its branches, thick and coarse as rope. This had always been my special hiding place—the spot where Atallah found me on the day Father announced the soldiers were coming.

Amid these vivid memories, Father's face appeared clearly—a younger face, loving yet stern, as it had been when he had lectured Rudah for bringing a gun home to protect us.

*The Jews and Palestinians are blood brothers,* he had said. *We must never forget that.*

Now, looking at Father's specially-grafted fig tree, I knew what those words meant. As a child, I had known that we got on well with the Jewish people from other villages, that we bartered with them and that the men occasionally enjoyed a rousing religious discussion. But with my seminary training, I was suddenly and keenly aware of St. Paul's declaration to the young churches: God had broken a dividing wall, and there was no longer "Jew nor Greek, slave nor free, male nor female;" in fact, all had become "Abraham's seed, and heirs according to God's promise" (Galatians 3:28-29). Further, Paul said, "not all who are descended from Israel are Israel . . . nor are they all Abraham's children . . . It is not only the natural children who are God's children, but also the children of the promise who are regarded as Abraham's offspring" (Romans 9:6-8). We Gentiles had been "grafted in" among God's chosen people of faith, just as Father had grafted six different kinds of fig trees together to make a delightful new tree. Beneath the rough bark where my hand rested, I knew that the living wood had fused together so perfectly that, should I cut the tree down, I could never see where one variety stopped and the other began.

How terribly sad that men could ignore God's plan for peace between divided brothers, even supporting one group as it wielded its might to force out the other. Such wrong thinking had divided the early Church, driving Hebrew and Gentile believers apart. I had been surprised at fellow seminarians and professors. They had often become furious in discussions when I had stated that Palestinians also had a God-given right to live in Israel, to sow and reap from the land, and to live as equals, not second-class citizens. Were we not "children of the promise, regarded as Abraham's offspring"?

Immediately, our discussions would swing in the direction of Old Testament prophecy. Again and again I was asked: "Did God not promise to regather the nation of Israel in their own homeland?"

The answer to that question was yes, of course. But that was not the only question, nor was it the main concern of the prophets. To address the full issue correctly, I had to start by asking another question: "To whom does God say the land really belongs?" And at once my friends would raise their eyebrows, wary that I was angling off the subject into some tricky, political double-talk. Not so, I was simply referring to the Old Testament Law wherein God says to the Jews:

. . . the land is mine and you are but aliens and tenants (Leviticus 25:23).

Quickly my friends would object, saying, "But God promised the land to Abraham, then to his son Isaac and also to Isaac's son Jacob who was renamed, Israel."

That was true, too. However, it is crucial to understand Abraham's response to so gracious a gift, of which he and his descendants were to be caretakers. He did not plow through the land, driving out its inhabitants, wielding power to establish his ownership by "right." Though he was to become the father of the faith for both Jews and Christians, he knew he was not the first inhabitant of Canaan to worship the one true God by any means. Melchizedek, the priest-king of Salem, once greeted Abraham with gifts of bread and wine and a message of welcome from God. Obviously, Melchizedek and his people had inhabited the land for some time before Abraham, honoring and worshiping God according to the old customs passed down from Noah and his fathers. Never did Abraham try to wrest Melchizedek's throne from him, nor did he take over anyone's land. He lived as a nomad. In fact, when his wife Sarah died, he very meekly *purchased* a cave in Hebron for her tomb.

Then I would ask a very crucial question: "What did God expect from the descendants of Abraham as caretakers dwelling in His land?"

It was to the Old Testament prophets that I turned for answers. In my own studies, I had become vibrantly aware that God had a special calling for his "caretaker people." In fact it was so high and hard a calling that I trembled to think of it: God demanded that they demonstrate His own character to the whole world, that they show forth the face of God in every action from the way they conducted their government down to the use of fair weights and measures in the marketplace. Often they failed miserably and, under God's judgment, they were broken apart by foreign powers such as the Babylonians. At last, God used the Romans to strike Israel and scatter the people throughout the nations.

Nonetheless, God would rescue them one last time after centuries of tremendous suffering. "Why?" I would ask my Christian friends. "Why would He continue to rescue a people He continually referred to as 'stiff-necked'?"

In answer, I would read from the ancient prophet Ezekiel. Speaking of this final rescue, with the powerful voice of the Lord, Ezekiel had delivered these blunt words to Israel:

> It is not for your sake, O house of Israel, that I am going to (gather you from all nations), but for the sake of my holy name, which you have profaned among the nations where you have gone. I will show the holiness of my great name, which has been profaned among the nations, the name you have profaned among them" (Ezekiel 36:22-23).

Here I would pause. Clearly God was acting in faithfulness to His own promises to the Jews; it was a reflection of His own eternally faithful nature, not a reward for human goodness. I always hastened to point out to my Christian friends that God had sent "a light to the gentiles," we who had lived in "great darkness," making us His sons though we, too, were undeserving of such honor.

And still there was a more vital reason why God would rescue the Jewish people once again—and presumably this rescue was taking place now in the twentieth century. I would continue reading, for Ezekiel had revealed God's true intent:

> "Then the nations will know that I am the Lord," declares the Sovereign Lord, "when I show myself holy through you before their eyes" (Ezekiel 36:23b).

Yes, there was something much more important at stake than a piece of land. God's true purpose in regathering Israel was to demonstrate to the world that He is holy and He leads a holy nation.

Likewise, the entire book of Isaiah rings with the same two-edged prophecy: God would comfort Israelites by delivering them from their persecutors among the nations *and* require them to live up to a high calling. They were not to exhibit a form of outward religiosity and then behave like any other nation. Even while promising to rescue them once again, God Himself denounced their old ways, saying that He had—

> "Looked for justice, but saw bloodshed; for righteousness, but heard cries of distress" (Isaiah 5:7).

Therefore Isaiah prophesied, God would not merely bring the Jews together again in a typical, secular state, He would

raise *a banner for the nations* and gather the
exiles of Israel; he will assemble the scattered people of Judah from the four quarters of the earth
(Isaiah 11:12, italics added).

There would be some in the coming years who would
popularize the interpretation of prophecy, writing books and
claiming that since Israel was now in its rightful place, all was
in readiness for the Second Coming of Christ. But to me, that
was an incomplete view of prophecy. For Isaiah, in his long
testimony, made it amply clear that God was requiring a true
change of heart in the Jewish people, a change in their
traditional exclusiveness which caused them to believe that
they alone were God's favored ones. All the prophets had
made it clear that such thinking led to pride and error and
wrong-doing. The new regathered Israel was to be different.
Isaiah records this command:

This is what the Lord says, "Maintain justice and
do what is right, for my salvation is close at hand
and my righteousness will soon be revealed.
Blessed is the man who does this. . . . Let no foreigner who has joined himself to the Lord say, 'The
Lord will surely exclude me from his people' . . .
for to them I will give within my temple and its walls
a memorial and a name *better than sons and
daughters;* I will give them an everlasting name that
will not be cut off. And foreigners who bind themselves to the Lord, to serve him, to love the name of
the Lord, and to worship him . . . these I will bring
to my holy mountain and give them joy in my house
of prayer' . . . . The Sovereign Lord declares—he
who gathers the exiles of Israel: "I will gather still

others to them besides those already gathered" (Isaiah 56:1-8).

I had sat down beneath the fig tree resting the back of my head against its knobby trunk as these prophecies flooded my thoughts again. Isaiah had always threaded justice and righteousness together throughout his prophecy. And clearly God intended to hold up His new Israel as a banner of justice before all the nations of the world. God's Israel included "foreigners," those who were not of the fleshly tribes of Israel, but who had been grafted into his family—just as the branches had been grafted into this fig tree. *And how sad,* I thought, *that we have been cut off like unwanted branches.*

Rising, I walked back to the car. I had another destination that morning. Weaving my way down the hills, past running springs and deep-green groves, I neared that other special place that I had been longing to visit—the Mount of Beatitudes.

As I drove, the voices of the ancient prophets still sounded. I found myself in hot debate, almost firing questions back at them. To me, as a Palestinian, Israel had returned to the land not in righteousness, but as my oppressor. As a Christian, I knew that I was grafted spiritually into the true family of Israel—though it certainly had not kept me or my people from suffering injustice. And how was I to respond? As a Christian, I had just as difficult a calling as a blood son of Israel. I could not join with the violent bands who were now attacking the country, even though I could feel their frustration. But neither could I live by the passive ways of Father and the other elders. Was my refusal to lay down and be trampled, to see our young people denied education, good jobs and decent homes, just my typical stubbornness? Many times I had felt guilty for my feelings, but I could no longer deny them.

At the Mount of Beatitudes, I parked in the visitors' lot. The Franciscans had built a replica of a Byzantine church on the mount, and nearby they provided a retreat house. At the moment, I was not eager to see tourists or any of the brothers, some of whom I knew. I followed the gravel pathways away from the buildings, out from the trees onto the open hillside overlooking the Sea of Galilee. As I ambled down a long flight of steps cut into the hill, I stopped, taken by the long vista of blue sea rimmed by hills on the east and west. The scene was unchanged since the days when Jesus toured Galilee on foot. Followed by a huge crowd of local people and others from Jerusalem, Judea and beyond the Jordan River, He had climbed up here to present His very first teaching to such a crowd. I could almost see them before me now.

A large group of women and children would have lingered in the background, as was the custom. In the forefront, spread across the grassy slope were the men. No doubt there were Jewish Zealots, those political activists who plotted the violent overthrow of the Roman occupation forces. Perhaps they hoped that Jesus would deliver a scorching message of destruction against the emperor. No doubt there were members of the Pharisee party, their long-tassled robes gathered about them, waiting to judge the orthodoxy cf Jesus—waiting to stone him if he stepped outside their rigid tenets. To the side were the peasants, the common tradesmen and some shepherds. Respectful, humble, they quietly listened for some uplifting word from this teacher—a message that would ease the burdens heaved on their backs by both the political fanatics and the grim-faced religious. Maybe there was among them a Samaritan, a despised outcast. As Jesus looked them over, he was already blending together the teachings of the Law and the Prophets with fresh vitalizing wisdom.

> And He began to teach them, saying: "Blessed are the poor in spirit, for theirs is the kingdom of heaven. ... ."

I was drawn in afresh by His words. Through the years they had become as part of my flesh. Perhaps their very familiarity had obscured their true meaning from me. For now, suddenly, with the voices of the ancient prophets still echoing in my head, Jesus' words seared through me for the first time with deep meaning.

The Beatitudes were prophecies! Not mere platitudes. Jesus' prophetic ministry had begun right there on the hill where I was standing. He had already set out to fulfill his purpose of grafting the Jews and Gentiles together into one family and one Kingdom by His death. Not the proud, but the "poor in spirit" would enter this coming kingdom where God's will would be done "on earth as it is in heaven."

Not all would welcome His idea of a Jewish and Gentile kingdom. Yet He knew so well the pain of oppression and loss. There would be suffering besides His own, and He told them—

> "Blessed are those who mourn, *for they will be comforted*. . . ."

The next prophecy amazed me.

> "Blessed are the meek, *for they will inherit the earth*. . . ."

Immediately, I thought of Moses who was called "the meekest man on earth." Yet he opposed Pharaoh and all Egypt, insisting upon freedom for God's people. Meekness then, was not weakness but relying fully upon God's power as Moses had.

And I was intrigued by Jesus' use of the word, "earth." From my seminary training in ancient languages, I knew that the Greek word was *ge,* and its counterpart in Hebrew was the word *'aretz*. It was the same word used by modern Jews in referring to Israel. They called it *Ha'aretz*: The Land. And it was the same term King David, whom Jesus was quoting, had used in a psalm of comfort:

> "Do not fret because of evil men or be envious of those who do wrong. . . . Trust in the Lord and do good. . . . A little while and the wicked will be no more. . . . But the meek will inherit *the land* and enjoy great peace" (Psalm 37:1,3,10,11).

Was Jesus really saying that the true sons of Israel, whether of Jewish or Gentile origin, had the God-given right to inhabit the land of Israel? According to God's promise through Isaiah—that He would give to the "foreigner . . . a name better than sons and daughters," and that He would "gather still others besides those already gathered"—it was true.

All these thoughts had rushed upon me so quickly, I stood silent and awed. If all this were true, what could I do about it? My imagination played over the faces of that long-ago crowd that had listened to Jesus. How could these nice-sounding words make any difference when an unjust military government held sway, sending dissidents to their death? When they lived in fear of a strict, unforgiving religious code?

The next words of Jesus struck me like lightning:

> "Blessed are those who hunger and thirst for righteousness, *for they will be satisfied.*"

Isaiah had bound *justice* and *righteousness* together. And Jesus, who often quoted Isaiah, surely knew that. In fact, it was for justice and righteousness that He had come. Over and over He demonstrated that the stiff laws of the Old Testament were only a shadow of the higher law of God's love that He had come to fulfill. The woman taken in adultery, when repentant, was not stoned, but forgiven for her weakness. The blind and the crippled were healed on the sabbath, "for the sabbath was made for man." The Samaritan outcast became a person worthy of honor and concern. For one of the first things Jesus did when He reconciled man to God was to restore human dignity.

The reason Jesus' words had struck me was this: Suddenly I knew that the first step toward reconciling Jew and Palestinian was the restoration of human dignity. Justice and righteousness were what I had been hungering and thirsting for. This was the third choice that ran like a straight path between violent opposition and calcified, passive non-resistance. If I were really committing my life to carry God's message to my people, I would have to lift up, as Jesus had, the men and women who had been degraded and beaten down. Only by regaining their shattered human dignity could they begin to be reconciled to the Israeli people, whom they saw as their enemies. This, I knew at once, went beyond all claims of land and rightful ownership; it was the true beginning.

As the passage ran through my head, another phrase sounded like the thunderclap after the lightning:

> "Blessed are the peacemakers, *for they will be called sons of God.*"

If I was to go out as a true servant of God and man, my first calling was to be a *peacemaker*. With these words, it seemed that I had finally found my way. I was oblivious that a deeper work was still needed in my heart.

At that moment, a busload of camera-laden tourists swarmed over the hillside, breaking into my reverie. No matter, for the direction now lay clear before me. Besides, the heat of the day was growing. As I hurried back to the car, I felt that the elusive thread of inner peace had once again been handed to me with the words of my Champion. As a boy, the things He had spoken on this mount had comforted me when I was accused of cutting the telephone wire to the nearby *kibbutz*. Now, as a young man on the verge of my life's work, these same powerfully simple words were guiding me again, giving me the peace of purpose and direction.

Slipping into the Volkswagen another image flickered in my head. Again there were crowds of people, this time in modern dress, and it was I who was delivering to them a message of love and hope and reconciliation. With each phrase their drooping shoulders raised a bit and on their despondent faces smiles broadened. God had not abandoned them to be second-class citizens, I said. He loved them. They had a right to live in this land and now it was time to be about the business of reconciliation with our Jewish brothers.

The Volkswagen fairly flew over the roads back to Nazareth. And in my heart—now bursting with plans and hope and ideals—I was flying, too.

A few weeks after my trip to the upper Galilee, I was summoned by the Bishop. I was nervous and excited and happy all at once, because I knew I was going to receive my first assignment. I had heard that Faraj had already received his assignment—a church in Nazareth.

"Elias," the Bishop announced to me brightly, "you are being sent to Ibillin in Galilee, a village of several thousand."

"Thank you, Bishop," I replied. "But—excuse me—I've never heard of Ibillin. Where is it located?"

"Oh, you'll have no trouble finding it," he hurried on. "We'll give you a map and some directions."

Then he paused. "Ehm . . . it is a rather small village. Modest. Maybe a little poor. The situation is—not easy. We thought that maybe you could try it for a month. No harm in that, is there? If it doesn't seem to work out, we'll have another look at your assignment."

Before I could comment, he continued. "I have already sent a letter to the Responsible of the church. They have been without a pastor there for some time. He is expecting you on August 15."

Abruptly the interview was over. I was ushered into the hall with a dozen or more unanswered questions on my mind.

It hardly mattered. The message of dignity for all and of reconciliation with our foes was still clarion-clear in my spirit. I would carry this message to my people. Throughout the first part of the summer, I prepared for the move to Ibillin, imagining how I would be welcomed by my first small "flock."

On the morning of August 15, even the blistering heat could not take the spring out of my step as I loaded the car and headed off to find Ibillin. There were so many small villages tucked in among the hills, if I got side-tracked or took a wrong turn. . . .

. . . I had been searching for hours when I finally turned onto a road that was little more than a dirt track, thinly paved with broken-up tar and gravel. On the highway north of Nazareth I had picked up a hitchhiking soldier who had assured me confidently that he knew just where Ibillin was. When I finally dropped him off outside his base, he had waved me on vaguely, saying, "This way. Just a little further." I had found myself in Tiberias, at the western edge of the country where a gas station attendant smiled sadly and shook his head, pointing me back toward Nazareth. I had driven out of my way for an hour and a half. Finally I was on the road to Ibillin—at the most, thirty minutes from Nazareth.

I pressed the accelerator and lurched up the steep road to the village, winding through groves of olive trees. Like most villages, Ibillin was perched on a hill. Poor-looking homes made of cinder block stood close to the road. Three or four children strayed in the path of my car, making me brake—beautiful boys and girls with dark hair and wide, wondering eyes. They were dressed in very poor clothes with no shoes, and they ignored my greeting. Several older men, their heads swathed with protective *kafiyehs*, stared at me sullenly when I waved at them. Suddenly I was aware of how little I knew about this village.

Near the top of the hill I drove into the churchyard. Wilted from the heat and the over-long trip, I was still eager to see the church. I had stepped out of the car in front of a decrepit-looking building, wondering where the parish house might be.

It was exciting: Here would begin my life's work.

A loud, angry voice distracted me.

Lunging toward me from the open door of the church came a middle-aged man, shouting and waving his arms. In that instant, too, I noticed that the church door was hanging almost off its hinges.

"Get out of here! Turn your car around and get out!" he bellowed, rushing at me menacingly.

Bewildered, I stumbled back against the car and blurted, "Excuse me. I'm Elias Chacour, the new—"

"I know exactly who you are," he interrupted. He was right in front of me now, shouting in my face. "I received the Bishop's letter saying that you were coming today."

I could hardly believe it. This volatile man was the Responsible of the church, the man who cared for the grounds and building and looked after financial matters—the man who was supposed to welcome me.

"We don't want you here," he ranted. "Do you understand? Go away!"

# 10

## Tough Miracles

Only a miracle of quick thinking—and some brashness—kept me from being pitched bodily out of Ibillin.

While the Responsible was still roaring in my face, I grabbed his hand reflexively. He must have thought I was going to shove him away, for his breath caught in mid-sentence and his jaw went slack. Where I got the nerve I hardly knew, but I blurted, "Let's pray together."

And there, leaning against the Volkswagen with the Responsible staring in disbelief, I opened my mouth, unsure of what would come out. "God, draw us together as Christian brothers. Help us work out our differences." What those differences were I could not fathom.

He was taken off guard only momentarily by my prayer. When I finished, he lunged ahead—though I noticed that his voice was less biting.

"If you think you're going to stay here you'd better go and bring back everything you priests have stolen from us."

The accusation staggered me. "What things? I was only ordained a few weeks ago. I didn't have time to steal anything."

"What things?" he mimicked me. "I'll show you 'what

things.'" And grabbing my sleeve, he jerked me toward the church.

The interior was dimly lit and cool. I was grateful—even if I was being dragged—to escape the mercilessly beating sun. But as my eyes adjusted, I was saddened at what I saw. The church was a sorry mess. The sagging door I had noticed was indeed hanging by one hinge. The interior was bare except for a few warped wooden benches. Left open to the elements, the walls were webbed with cracks and the paint was peeled and scaley. The fine frescoes that had decorated the walls were reduced to flakes of colored plaster. And at the front, once-fine draperies hung faded, dusty and limp.

As I took in this shambles, speechless, the Responsible rambled on with his accusations against the previous pastor: He had virtually disappeared one night several years before, taking with him the cup and plate used in Communion, most of the benches and even the outdoor toilet.

Then, grabbing my sleeve again, he pulled me back out into the blazing afternoon sun to show me the "parish house." As I feared, it was the small, decrepit-looking building in front of which I had parked.

"*If* you stay," he remarked with noticeable emphasis, "this is where you'll live."

A quick inspection of the building's two small rooms revealed the presence of a greasy stove, the absence of a bed— and no bathroom facilities at all, since the outdoor privy had gone off with my predecessor. A battered kerosene lamp, the only source of light, sat at the edge of a three-legged table. The only water for washing, drinking or cooking was cold and came from a leaky outdoor spigot. When the Bishop advised me that Ibillin would be "a challenge," he certainly had not wasted his breath on details. I kept trying to comfort myself, thinking, *One month—it's only for a month.*

Turning to the Responsible, who was watching me slyly, I

smiled and said, "This is suitable. Just fine. I'll be staying."
He lingered only long enough to watch me haul my suitcases
from the car, then he left in disgust. I tried to settle in, moving
benches from the church for my bed. Fleetingly, the thought
came to me that Ibillin might be the perfect place for me, my
first small experiment in becoming a peacemaker. I shoved
that idea away. I would make the best of it—just for four
weeks.

What I learned about Ibillin in the next few days was
pathetic. For, like the church, the village itself was in a
decline. Ibillin, I discovered, was an old, old settlement, one
of whose citizens was a Church father who played a master-
ful role in the Counsel of Nicea in 325 A.D. In the ensuing
centuries, the village was a battlefield for Crusader and
Islamic armies. The infamous Salah-al-din, or "Saladin,"
had constructed a stone fortress nearby, and his scimitar-
wielding forces had poured blood over these hills. Though
the light of Christianity flickered, it could not be quenched
and the Church remained strong until the twentieth century.

It was only in the upheavals of the 1940s, when families
were scattered and resettled, that Ibillin's ancient social
fabric tore apart. In the confusion of war, Moslems, Greek
Orthodox and Melkite Christians were slammed together. A
mosque, an Orthodox sanctuary and our own church now
clutched at the top of the same hill—each group vying for
power and influence in Ibillin. The divisions were disastrous.
Among the problems—such as delinquency and alco-
holism—the village counsels could never agree on a solution
to the village's antiquated, inadequate water supply. So nothing was accomplished and hatred spread.

Even families were hotly divided over issues. One of the
most tragic cases was the family where four brothers—one of
whom was the village policeman—detested each other so
vehemently that people rushed off the streets when they saw

two of them walking toward each other. It hurt me deeply to learn that these brothers were believers, once active in the church.

The most distressing thing was the vicious hatred of the Christians I had come to serve. The church was so blasted apart by hostility that only a handful of believers ever came to prayer. Primarily, there was disappointment that the church leadership avoided issues of justice and equality and seemed to court the new government that fought against us. Rather than face the Zionists, the bishops and archbishops seemed more interested in preserving their shrines—the "holy stones"—and did not speak out. The final blow had come from the previous pastor, who, when confronted with a divided, poverty-cursed situation, simply disappeared. Little wonder that the Responsible detested me for all that I represented. Little wonder that hopelessness had dulled faith.

Whatever wounds the Church heirarchy and the previous pastor had inflicted, the Responsible only aggravated matters. By visiting with a few neighbors—reluctant as they were to see me—I discovered, too, that the Responsible ruled with an iron will. He had assumed power, declaring who was welcome in the church and who was not. Most people were *not*. He was forceful and no one dared oppose him.

Perhaps that was the challenge that nudged me. The Responsible wanted to see me leave after only one month. I would stay longer—maybe a few months, maybe even a year.

At once I determined to visit every family in Ibillin, whether they were Christian or not. To me, it was an unmistakable opportunity to bear the love of the cross into this shattered place that was perched between the star of David and the crescent of Mohammed. Enthusiastically, I began knocking on doors every afternoon, telling families that they were welcome at the church again. Since hospitality is a quality so deeply ingrained by our culture I was never turned away, but was always treated to coffee and fruits and some of their carefully hoarded sweets. A few men even volunteered to make new benches and fix the broken church doors. Still, most were reluctant to come back to the church, strangely reluctant even to talk about it. And with the size of the village, I could see that it was going to be a time-consuming task to reach every family. I needed help.

One afternoon some, weeks after my one-month trial period had ended, I left off my visits long enough to drive to Nazareth. I hoped to see an old friend, a deeply spiritual woman known as Mother Josephate who headed a community of Christian women. These sisters lived simply, dedicating themselves to prayer—but would any of them be willing to leave their community and work amid the poor conditions of Ibillin with me?

Mother Josephate greeted me warmly, her lovely, aged face radiating a compassion that seemed to me more than mere human love. Graciously, she listened to my story about the problems in Ibillin and to my plea for two women from her community to come and help—even if only for a day at a time—by visiting the women of the village.

When I had finished she replied, "I believe that this request comes not from you, but from the heart of God. I'm sure some will want to go with you. Nevertheless, before I can promise you the help of two sisters, I must get the approval of our superior."

I knew that was true, since hers was a Roman community and tightly governed by their heirarchy. We agreed that I would return to Nazareth in several weeks—though Mother Josephate assured me in her kind way that there would be no problem. It was just a formality, a matter of submission and obedience on her part.

Before I saw Mother Josephate again, I found out why the people of Ibillin had been so reluctant even to talk about coming to church again. The Responsible learned that I was visiting in homes—and he became infuriated. The previous pastor had rarely bothered with home visits. Now the Responsible was jealous and suspicious of me, whom he considered a brash, obnoxious young man unfit for my calling. He began to dog me constantly, opposed my visiting certain people that he, for whatever obtuse reason, disliked.

There was one man for whom the Responsible had an absolutely irrational hatred. That was Habib, a gentle man who lived right next to the parish house. Habib often spoke out against the annexation of remaining Palestinian farmland by the Israeli government, a practice that was increasing at an alarming rate. The Responsible slandered him, calling him a dirty communist, and did not allow him even to set foot on church property.

Without question, the Responsible had a killing choke-hold on the church. It had to be broken. On the other hand, the people were distrustful of anyone representing the Church. I could not simply shove the Responsible aside—in that way, I would look like one more power-grasping tyrant. I could not start an ugly argument. Yet a confrontation was coming and it would either split the believers of Ibillin irreparably or it would unite them.

Nightly, as the wooden benches stiffened my neck and bruised my hips, I imagined Jesus faced with the warring factions of His day. I thought of the Pharisees, raising their eyebrows judgmentally as He approached a prostitute, or a publican. What would He do?

One afternoon, on one of the last warm days of summer, I knew what *I* had to do. The Responsible was still dogging me on my rounds, still treating me as if I were his puppet and expecting me to dance with every twitch of the strings. Something had to break.

We stepped out of the parish house into the walled-in yard that surrounded it. The Responsible was right at my heels. The yard was supposed to be a garden. Sadly, it was as barren as the church—a patch of weeds. Once again the Responsible was beginning to dictate who I would see, and I knew this was the moment.

"I think I will visit Habib today," I remarked casually, looking up at Habib's home which could be seen beyond the garden wall.

"No. You will *not* see him!" the Responsible snapped.

I tossed up my hands. "All right. I'm not going to argue with you."

Surely he thought I was surrendering. A self-satisfied grin played at the corners of his mouth. I pressed my advantage.

"Will you wait here for me? Just for a moment?" I asked innocently. "I have something to take care of before I go with you. And I know this won't interest you at all."

Appeased and off guard, he agreed.

I stepped out of the garden into the street alone. Once the gate slammed shut, I hurried along beside the wall, turning in at the outside stairway that led up to Habib's second-floor apartment. As I mounted the steps, I could see down into the church garden—and I could *be seen* as well. The Responsible spotted me immediately, and even from a distance, I saw the color rising in his face.

Before he could shout at me, I called out pleasantly: "I knew you would feel uncomfortable visiting here. So I didn't force you to come with me. You can relax and wait if you like. I won't be long."

As it turned out, that was untrue. Habib and I found such a ready kinship of spirit that I quickly lost track of time. I was

charmed by his knowledge of agriculture, his love for the soil
and growing things which reminded me of Father. And besides his knowledge about trees and grapevines, Habib knew
the New Testament thoroughly. It distressed me that such a
person had been shunned and badly treated by the Church. I
promised myself—and Habib—that this was just the first of
many visits and, of course, I invited him to the church.
Understandably, he did not accept the invitation at once, but
I knew we would be fast friends.

As he saw me out the door, I glanced at my watch and
started. *Two hours* had passed, and I had promised the
Responsible I would return in a few minutes. Uneasily, I
walked down the stairs from Habib's apartment, scanning
the empty churchyard.

Thankfully, the Responsible had given up and gone home.
Nor did he confront me when next I saw him. I would
continue to see Habib, quietly so it would not become an
issue. Yet I knew by the Responsible's bitter silence that it
was only a matter of time.


Some weeks passed, and again I drove to Nazareth. The
sooner I had help from the Christian sisters, the faster I
could reach out to all the families of Ibillin. I had even begun
to tramp the streets each Sunday morning for two hours
before the church service began, knocking on doors and
reminding the believers that our church was not *the* Church
without them. It was tiring, ceaseless work, and I was desperate for some support. Eagerly, I bounded into Mother
Josephate's office to keep our appointment.

One look at her face, and I knew that all was not right.
Seated behind her desk, she folded her hands carefully,
cleared her throat and picked a cautious path with her words.

"You know the difficult position I am in. I've always
supported my superior's authority. After all, he has been

placed over me by the Church." Here she stopped, pursing her lips before delivering the hard words. "I asked his permission to let two sisters work with you in Ibillin—and he denied my request."

My heart felt empty as she relayed their conversation. Her superior had asked if any families in Ibillin were Roman Catholic. When Mother Josephate said no, he asked if any might convert. Patiently, she told him that conversion was not the point. "In that case," he said peremptorily, "you cannot send two sisters there."

I supposed that was the end of the matter. With a heavy sigh, I was about to thank Mother Josephate and leave. As I started to rise, she motioned for me to sit.

"I told you I am in a difficult situation. That's true. But I have to answer to a higher authority than my superior or the Church. I have to answer to God, and I can't blame my superior if I fail to do what is right." And now I saw the familiar glimmer in her eyes again, a mischievous compassionate smile. "I was forbidden to send 'two' sisters—and so I am going to send *three*."

I was thrilled. Even more, I was moved with the deepest gratitude. Mother Josephate had struggled with this decision, I knew. She would never flippantly defy her superiors but was acting on a heart-set conviction. I squeezed her hand, thanking her over and over. We were like two sparks, I thought—not quite enough to set Ibillin afire, but there was the faint promise of brightness in my work now.

And the promise proved to be faint enough, indeed.

The very next Sunday, I drove to Nazareth again to pick up the three sisters Mother Josephate had recruited. When I arrived at their residence I was prepared to meet my three eager, enthusiastic workers.

At the door, Mother Josephate greeted me, introducing the volunteers. Mère Macaire, the eldest, seemed the strong, politely commanding type. However, a cough that shook her whole frame told me she was in poor health. Ghislaine was a short, cheerfully plump woman with graying hair and wistful, pale eyes. She looked like the universal grand-mother. The third, Nazarena, was younger and darker. Her skin was a smooth, rich olive tone, and she was thin almost to the point of frailty. What these three had in common, besides the gray outfits of their community, was the wary-eyed, sullen way they stared at me. One look told me they were far less than enthusiastic.

We marched out to the car together and as I opened the door for them, Mère Macaire demanded, "You *are* going to return us here right after your service—is that right?"

I was dismayed. It was not my intent to ferry them back and forth from Nazareth to Ibillin just to have warm bodies sitting in church. I was about to close the car door and think up some polite way to get out of this arrangement. I was busy enough in Ibillin without taking on extra driving. But there was Mother Josephate, smiling at me from the doorway. I could not refuse her graciousness, and so, hardly flinching, I replied, "Yes. I'll return you immediately."

To my sheer amazement, when I deposited them back at the convent that afternoon, Mère Macaire insisted that I come for them the following Sunday. The next Sunday it was the same and the week after that. It was quite confusing to me since they showed little outward interest in the people of Ibillin, but kept to themselves all during the service. And afterwards, they marched straight out to the car, waiting with tight-lipped faces for me to say goodbye to the two dozen villagers who were now reluctantly coming to the church. I fully expected each Sunday to be their last—and sometimes I secretly hoped it would be. When I hinted that they might stay and talk to the village women, they were silent. Still, they came faithfully each week as winter settled about us.

The reason for their strange persistence—and their seeming indifference—became clear to me one day several months into their "volunteer work." Mother Josephate cornered me one afternoon, asking if all was going well with the sisters. I tried to answer politely without lying outright. She saw through my words at once.

"Don't give up on them," she said wistfully. "They have a 'convent mentality.' It happens for some. Everything is regulated by the clock. There is a time to eat, to pray, to sleep—a time to close the door and turn people away. They will change though. Be patient. They have good hearts or they would never go with you."

I learned in that conversation, too, that many in the Church considered the villages of the Galilee tough places to work. They were poor, the populations were mixed with Christians, Moslems, and also many Druze whose faith blended together Christianity, Islam and Judaism. And though Christ Himself traveled and taught and performed miracles of love in these villages, many Church people preferred to huddle safely and comfortably around the holy shrines.

The week following our conversation, I decided to help the sisters change a little faster. After church I simply refused to take them back to the convent immediately. Instead, I had a modest lunch prepared—the best I could do. I had also told some village women that the sisters would be staying and that they had minor skills in nursing. Since colds and viruses attacked their children savagely during these bitter, rainy months, the women were elated.

Before we could set the table for lunch there was a knock at the parish house door. I ran to answer it, for an icy drizzle was spattering the streets. When I opened the door, a young mother stepped timidly inside, cradling a blanketed bundle in her arms. Her face was tense, fearful. She lifted the folds of the blanket and inside was a very small boy about two years old. His curly, dark hair was damp, not from rain, but from fever.

"His name is Ibrahim," said the mother. "You know, like Father Abraham."

To my delight the sisters did not hesitate a moment, but swarmed around the woman comforting her, clucking over the child. Nazarena, who knew the most about nursing, took the listless child on her lap, gently rocking him as she stroked his hot, moist forehead. Ghislaine hurried to the stove to make some hot tea. Mère Macaire fussed over the young woman, asking questions about the boy's illness. I watched the mother, swaddled in such sudden care and affection, as every trace of fear drained from her face.

Standing quietly aside, I could not help but think that this poor child had been sent by God. It was one thing for the sisters to meet unfamiliar men and women in church. It was quite another matter to sit a sick child on their laps. Each time Ibrahim looked up into Nazarena's face, his dark eyes glassy and pain-filled, I sensed that the powerful, wordless bond between woman and child was forming. In that rare way that women have, all three sisters became Ibrahim's mother that day.

The sisters were alight with plans for the next week's trip as I drove them home. They would bring cold medicines and aspirins in case others were sick. I smiled and drove on silently.

Though the sisters tacitly refused to go into the homes, their new contact with the people of Ibillin brought an unexpected benefit. Since my arrival the previous summer, an occasional batch of flatbread would be delivered to the doorstep, a few pieces of fruit, or a basket of vegetables. After the sisters began dispensing their nursing care, food began arriving every day of the week. Increasingly, I received gifts of cheese, milk, eggs, oranges, meats, cakes, bread, olives, honey, coffee—all from the grateful hearts of Ibillin.

Somewhere during this time, I realized my own growing love for this village. My one-month trial period had gone on for almost six months and I could not think of leaving. I was still sleeping on a hard bench. The village and even the church were still rife with hatred. But I was seeing past the hardships and divisions. Perhaps it was the joyful eyes of the mothers bringing their babies for the sisters to doctor and for me to bless. Or the bands of older boys—young men, really—who milled about restlessly on the street corners. Or the shy, sweet faces of girls who demurely served coffee when I visited their fathers at home. Beneath the surface of Ibillin— a surface cracked by religious, social and political tensions, toughened by poor conditions—were tender, timidly opening hearts. Hearts of common people who did not want division, but peace. Men who once passed me on the streets with hostile indifference would pump my hand, grateful for some small ministration that the sisters had performed for a son or daughter. Gradually, I sensed that something was happening here. If so, it was not like the instant, powerful signs performed by Jesus—it would be a tough miracle.

Beneath this surface, too, opposition to my presence in Ibillin was building.

While I was busy with my afternoon and Sunday morning rounds, the Responsible had been gathering support for his cause also. Winter and spring passed, and as the summer of 1966 approached, I could sense that the many factions in the divided church were lining up on two sides—the Responsible's and mine. Others in the village were taking sides, too. I was horrified when this occurred to me and more than a little uneasy that the odds were in his favor. What chance did a young man of twenty-six—an outsider—stand against a lifetime village resident, and a powerful one at that? A head-to-head collision, the very thing I dreaded, seemed unavoidable.

The confrontation came on an early fall morning more than eighteen months after my arrival.

I answered an impatient pounding at my door to find the Responsible and half a dozen other men staring at me sullenly. "Come with us," the Responsible demanded without explanation. Dutifully, I stepped outside and followed.

They marched me around back to the parish house garden where the Responsible pointed accusingly at a young vine that was twining around some posts. "What is this?" he asked belligerently.

"It's a grapevine," I replied.

"Who planted it here?"

I had a sinking feeling. "My neighbor, Habib," I responded. The past spring, after I had reminisced to Habib about my childhood hideout in the vine-laced tree in Biram, he had surprised me with this gift of a hybrid grapevine. It promised to dress up the brown, barren garden.

"If Habib planted it, then it must go," the Responsible raved. "He has no right here, and I don't want him to have any excuse to come onto this property. Tear out the vine!"

I thrust my chin out stubbornly. Anger and exasperation boiled up inside. My thoughts blistered with accusations of *stupidity, small-mindedness*. And at the same moment, amazingly, a small, almost unheard voice somewhere inside prayed, *Father, let me speak with your tongue, not my own*.

Almost before I knew what I was saying, I replied evenly, "Bring me a bucket of water."

Triumphantly, the Responsible sent one of his men hunting for a bucket, supposing I meant to loosen the soil so the vine could be uprooted. When the man returned, lugging water from the outdoor spigot, I had only just determined what to do with it.

He thrust it into my hands, and I stooped, spilling water over the leaves in slow, ritual fashion. Setting the empty bucket aside, I raised my right hand over the vine. In as serious an intonation as I could manage, I said, "I baptize you in the name of the Father, and of the Son, and of the Holy Spirit. Amen."

The men stared at me as if I were dangerously insane. "There," I addressed them warmly, "now this is a Christian vine. You cannot uproot your own brother. So he stays."

Indignantly, they turned on their heels and stomped away.

For the moment we were stalemated. I knew, however, that the bitter hostilities within the church and in Ibillin could not be resolved by mere cleverness. I realized, as I plodded through the days ahead, that the skill of a surgeon was needed to cut away the sick thing that was destroying this village—not suspecting that I would be the first to come under the surgeon's knife.

Early in 1967, the sisters surprised me with an announcement.

"We would like to come and live in Ibillin," Mère Macaire declared one Sunday as we drove out of Nazareth. Ghislaine and Nazarena nodded. "That is," Mère Macaire added, "if you will have us."

I could have kissed them. More appropriately I responded, not wanting to sound over-eager, "Certainly. When?"

I don't know how Mother Josephate convinced her superior, but the three sisters moved to Ibillin the very next week. I knew it would be tough on them, since Mère Macaire was old and had health problems and Nazarena, too, was a bit frail. Besides which, there was a problem with living arrangements. We were able to find three metal-framed beds for the sisters, but we could not all share the parish house. Since no other quarters were offered, I was forced to sleep in the car. In a letter to Lony and Franz, I jokingly thanked them for giving me my "bedroom-on-wheels."

Despite the bitter, cramping cold, I was glad that the sisters willingly received visitors all week now. Cheerily, I stepped up my own pace, visiting in the homes of Christian and Moslem families alike. It was during this time that my painful surgery of the spirit took place.

Late one night toward the end of winter, a message came that a certain woman in the church was dying. She was quite old and had been very ill, so I was not surprised. However, two things disturbed me deeply. First, I had never before attended someone at the door of death. Second, this woman was the mother of the four feuding brothers and it was to the home of the oldest—the village policeman, whose name was Abu Mouhib—that I was called.

Nervously, I hurried out into the moonless night. I groped my way blindly through the dark village, fearful that I would not get to the woman before she died. Or perhaps I feared that I would.

When I finally reached the home of Abu Mouhib, where the woman had been residing, I was shaking visibly. He hesitated a moment before allowing me to enter. He disliked me, I knew, though he did come to church on rare occasions. This was not the time to express personal dislikes, however, and he showed me to his mother's sickroom.

Far into the dark morning hours I sat with the dying woman, whispering a few timid words of comfort. Those years in seminary had failed to prepare me for this. In my sweating palm lay her tremorous, blue-veined hand. It was cold and curled up like an alabaster leaf. Her breathing came in rasps for an hour or so—and then it ceased. With icy fingers, I closed her eyes.

My legs were rubber when I told Abu Mouhib that his mother was dead. Trying the best I could to comfort, I offered to go and tell his three brothers. "They would like to come and see her, I'm sure."

Abu Mouhib's grieving features stiffened into a scowl. "No!" he shouted. "My brothers do not set foot in my house. If they dare to come here you will have five funerals on your hands, because we will kill each other."

A chill shook me. Even the death of their mother would not draw these brothers together. As I helped wrap the woman's frail body, I grieved for her—for her sons, and for the whole village.

A gray, faint light lit the streets as I made my way back home. A deadening exhaustion stooped my shoulders. I wanted only to crawl into my Volkswagen and sleep for hours and hours. As I squeezed myself into the back seat, however, I felt a real ache of grief in my chest—grief and anger. Sleep would not come.

I lay there wrestling against the whole world of conflict that sprawled around me. In my head, I lunged at the four brothers in an angry conversation, telling them how disgusted I was at their behavior. Couldn't they forgive each other now when they needed to honor their own mother?

And they were not the only ones I attacked. The image of the Responsible smirked at me in the half-light, and I flung hard words in his face. I railed at the priest who had stolen from the church; at fellow seminarians who had slandered all Palestinians, calling us "terrorists;" at seminary professors; at the principal who had punished me at the school in Nazareth.

Another image appeared vividly . . . a military policeman

towering over a small boy, whipping him with a stick . . . I
heard cries . . . my own voice . . . I was picking up a stick,
beating, smashing the man's head until he fell unconscious
. . . bleeding . . . There were tanks on the hills of Biram . . .
explosions . . . our homes stood fast while the tanks blew
apart . . . and the agonized bodies of soldiers. . . .

Then I knew.

Silent, still, I lay there, aware for the first time that I was
capable of vicious, killing hatred. Aware that all men everywhere—despite the thin, polite veneer of society—are capable of hideous violence against other men. Not just the
Nazis, or the Zionists or the Palestinian commandos—but
me. I had covered my hurts with Christian responses, but
inside the anger had gnawed. With this sudden, startling view
of myself, a familiar inner voice spoke firmly, without compromise: *If you hate your brother you are guilty of murder.*
Now I understood.

I was aware of other words being spoken. A Man was dying
a hideous death at the hands of His captors—a Man of Peace,
who suffered unjustly—hung on a cross. *Father forgive
them*, I repeated. *And forgive me, too.*

In that moment, forgiveness closed the long-open gap of
anger and bitterness inside me. From the time I had been
beaten as a small boy, I had denied the violence inside me.
Now . . . the taming hand that had taught me compassion on
the border of West Germany had finally stilled me enough to
see the deep hatred in my own soul.

Physically and emotionally spent, I fell asleep. Later that
morning, I woke with a new, clean feeling of calmness. The
change that had begun on my visit to the Mount of Beatitudes
was complete. I knew what I must do in Ibillin.

My year-and-a-half of home visits and the sisters' months
of ministrations had made a dent—a small dent—in reuniting

the believers of Ibillin. Few attended the church regularly and walls of hostile silence remained firm. However, most of them would not think of missing services during the Christmas and Easter seasons, coming to be comforted by familiar customs, not out of desire for true spiritual renewal. True to the pattern, attendance increased markedly on the first Sunday of Lent, growing each week as Easter approached.

On Palm Sunday, every bench was packed. Nearly the entire congregation had come, plus a few other villagers whom I had invited. The weather that morning was balmy, with a warm, light wind straying through the streets, so I left the doors wide open, hoping that passers-by might be attracted by our singing. When I stood up, raising my hands to signal the start of the service, I was jolted by stark, staring faces.

Looks of open hostility greeted me. The Responsible's faction was clustered on one side of the church, almost challenging me with their icy glares. Indifferently, those whom the Responsible had ostracized sat on the opposite side. I was amazed to see Abu Mouhib, the policeman, perched in the very front row with his wife and children. In each of the other three quadrants of the church, as distant from one another as possible, were his three brothers. The sisters, I could tell, felt the tension, too, for their faces were blanched. I rose and began the first hymn, certain that no one would be attracted by our pathetically dismal singing. I thought, with sadness, of the battle lines that were drawn across the aisles of that sanctuary. And nervously, I hoped that no one would notice the odd lump in the pocket beneath my vestment.

What followed was undoubtedly the stiffest service, the most unimpassioned sermon of my life. The congregation endured me indifferently, fulfilling their holiday obligation to warm the benches. But then, they did not suspect what was coming. At the close of the liturgy, everyone rose for the benediction. I lifted my hand, my stomach fluttering, and paused. It was now or never.

Swiftly, I dropped my hand and strode toward the open doors at the back of the church. Every eye followed me with curiosity. I drew shut the huge double doors which workmen had rehung for me. From my pocket I pulled a thick chain, laced it through the handles and fastened it firmly with a padlock.

Returning to the front, I could almost feel the temperature rising. Or was it just me? Turning to face the congregation, I took a deep breath.

"Sitting in this building does not make you a Christian," I began awkwardly. My voice seemed to echo too loudly in the shocked silence. The sisters' eyes were shut, their lips moving furiously in prayer.

"You are a people divided. You argue and hate each other—gossip and spread malicious lies. What do the Moslems and the unbelievers think when they see you? Surely that your religion is false. If you can't love your brother that you see, how can you say you love God who is invisible? You have allowed the body of Christ to be disgraced."

Now the shock had turned to anger. The Responsible trembled and seemed as though he was about to choke. Abu Mouhib tapped his foot angrily and turned red around the collar. In his eyes, though, I thought I detected something besides anger.

Plunging ahead, my voice rose. "For many months, I've tried to unite you. I've failed, because I'm only a man. But there is someone else who can bring you together in true unity. His name is Jesus Christ. He is the one who gives you power to forgive. So now I will be quiet and allow Him to give you that power. If you *will not* forgive, we will stay locked in here. You can kill each other and I'll provide your funerals gratis."

Silence hung. Tight-lipped, fists clenched, everyone glared at me as if carved from stone. I waited. With agonizing slowness, the minutes passed. Three minutes . . . five . . . ten . . . I could hear, outside, a boy coaxing his donkey up the street and the slow *clop-clop* of its hooves. Still no one flinched. My breathing had become shallow and I swallowed hard. *Surely I've finished everything*, I chastised myself, *undone all these months of hard work with my*—Then a sudden movement caught my eye.

Someone was standing. Abu Mouhib rose and faced the congregation, his head bowed, remorse shining in his eyes. With his first words, I could scarcely believe that this was the same hard-bitten policeman who had treated me so brusquely.

"I am sorry," he faltered. All eyes were on him. "I am the worst one of all. I've hated my own brothers. Hated them so much I wanted to kill them. More than any of you I need forgiveness."

And then he turned to me. "Can you forgive me, too, Abuna?"

I was amazed! *Abuna* means "our father," a term of affection and respect. I had been called other things since arriving in Ibillin, but nothing so warm.

"Come here," I replied, motioning him to my side. He came, and we greeted each other with the kiss of peace. "Of course I forgive you," I said. "Now go and greet your brothers."

Before he was halfway down the aisle, his three brothers had rushed to him. They held each other in a long embrace, each one asking forgiveness of the others.

In an instant the church was a chaos of embracing and repentance. Cousins who had not spoken to each other in years, wept together openly. Women asked forgiveness for malicious gossip. Men confessed to passing damaging lies about each other. People who had ignored the sisters and myself in the streets now begged us to come to their homes. Only the Responsible stood quietly apart, accepting only stiffly my embrace. This second church service—a liturgy of love and reconciliation—went on for nearly a full hour.

In the midst of these joyful reunions, I recalled Father's words when he had told us why we must receive the Jews from Europe into our home. And loudly, I announced: "We're not going to wait until next week to celebrate the Resurrection. Let's celebrate it now. We were dead to each other. Now we are alive again."

I began to sing. This time our voices joined as one, the words binding us together in a song of triumph: "Christ is risen from the dead. By His death He has trampled death and given life to those in the tomb."

Even then it did not end. The momentum carried us out of the church and into the streets where true Christianity belongs. For the rest of the day and far into the evening, I joined groups of believers as they went from house to house throughout Ibillin. At every door, someone had to ask forgiveness for a certain wrong. Never was forgiveness withheld. Now I knew that inner peace could be passed from man to man and woman to woman.

As I watched, I recalled, too, an image that had come to me as a young boy in Haifa. Before my eyes, I was seeing a ruined church rebuilt at last—not with mortar and rock, but with living stones.

## *11*

## *Bridges or Walls?*

Truly the church in Ibillin resembled a lifeless body returning from the dead. In the jubilant singing and prayers on
Easter, I felt the eager breath of new life. In the streaming
tears, I saw, as in the story of Lazarus, brothers and sisters
rushing to each other's embrace. Gifts of food arrived daily
and, amazingly, we never purchased groceries from then on,
for the generosity of these humble people was to prove
bottomless. Immediately after the holiday, some in the congregation decided that the church building itself needed total
rejuvenation and the sanctuary was soon bustling with workmen busy at repairs.

Mornings, I laced my way through the maze of ladders and
drop-cloths inside the church, directing the renovations.
Carpenters patched the crumbling plaster; painters recoated
the walls and woodwork; electricians ferreted through the
walls to fix frayed wiring. Plans were being made to enlarge
the parish house so that I could have a small apartment,
which pleased me greatly.

These signs, I realized, were only cosmetic. I knew that
for a body to live, it would take nurturing. Afternoons, I kept
up a busy schedule of home visits, breaking the bread of

friendship to strengthen those delicate, new ties. And I knew that another step was vital if Ibillin was to become a village reconciled with itself.

One evening, several weeks after Easter, the sisters and I were seated at the table in our small, makeshift kitchen. Mère Macaire set a steaming plate of hot bread, eggs, potatoes and mint before me. In the eighteen months since they had come to Ibillin, these three women had become mother-like in caring for me. As was our custom, we paused for prayer before eating and the sisters bowed their heads.

"Sisters," I began startling them out of their routine, "I have a question for you. If Jesus Christ Himself was somewhere out in the streets of Ibillin needing our help, what would you do?

They stared at me. The answer was obvious: They would hurry to find Him.

"Well, I have great news for you ladies," I beamed. "Jesus Himself is *not* in Ibillin—but He has sent others and He wants to see if we will help them instead. Whatever we do to the *least* of men, we do for Him. And the person He sends may not be Christian, but Moslem. Jesus does not ask us just to preach to Moslems, but first to show His love. Will you go to them, too?

"We can't wait for people to see things our way—to believe and talk and act like us. Isn't it more important to demonstrate the *spirit* of the gospel, rather than battering people with the words? If we are going to represent our God to the Moslems, we have to choose. Do we build bridges . . . or walls?"

Even as I lectured them, I was soon to be confronted with a similar choice—building bridges or walls—and it would not be as easy as I was making it sound.

The sisters, for their part, needed no further prodding. They began the very next day to visit Moslem women a home. They were wonderfully received, and, in the end, it was the mutual love for children that bridged the gap between our religions. Soon the sisters were teaching the young women sewing, tailoring and baking, and they invited these girls to Bible classes they held for our church young people. In a short time, they asked my approval to start a kindergarten in the parish house—a school for their "babies."

News about the sisters' tender concern for Moslem and Christian alike spread immediately through the hill country. Almost overnight, other villages began contacting me, asking that I send Christian women to live with them, to work and teach. I had not expected this. Moreover, I was amazed that so tiny a spark of love could shine like a beacon. Before I could begin to make arrangements, however, I was brought up short. In May, I was summoned by the Bishop.

With a broad, friendly grin, he floored me with this unwelcome announcement: "You, Elias, are going to study at the Hebrew University in Jerusalem. I made some contacts, and you are to be the very first Palestinian priest they have ever accepted. An honor—a true honor. All the arrangements are made. You leave in two weeks."

"To study? Why?" I nearly shouted. "I have my work in Ibillin—where you sent me. Good things are happening."

"Elias," he said, bristling. "do you know how embarrassing it is for me when I talk to rabbis? I'm amazed at their knowledge of the New Testament—and we don't know half as much about the Old Testament. I'm sending you because you were a top student in seminary. Besides you already know Hebrew and Aramaic."

I bridled inwardly. The church had changed so much in the few months since our Palm Sunday renewal. The services were growing weekly, with young and old uniting in prayers and hymns. It would take time for some people, like Habib who had been so badly slandered, to feel comfortable visit-

ing the church again. Only a few, like the Responsible refused to come back.

"So. It's all set. You will go," he concluded, ushering me
out of his office.

As I returned to Ibillin, I was upset. I had just seen the first
breakthrough toward reconciling people in this divided land.
The believers were starting to trust the Church heirarchy
again. And now I was being sent away.

Not to mention another important development among the
villages of Galilee. In recent months a small group of young
men from Biram had banded together to rebuild our ruined
Church of Notre Dame as a symbol of hope for Palestinian
people. Young men came from all the villages where we had
been scattered, giving time and muscle power. I had gone
with them, laboring, too.

Now all these things—the church in Ibillin, the other
needy villages and the reconstruction efforts—would have to
wait. I only had time for a few hasty preparations, setting up
a church council to govern in my absence and helping the
sisters to establish their kindergarten—all with a measure of
discouragement and uneasiness.

Neither the Bishop nor I could foresee the incredible, far-
reaching impact of my years at the Hebrew University.

Spring 1967 could not have been a better time—or a worse
one—to plan a move to Jerusalem, the "city of peace." It was
a pivotal moment in the history of modern Israel.

Economically, Israel was in rapid decline. So much money
was needed for defense alone that inflation was growing
cancerously and soon would top one hundred percent an-
nually. Socially, the hope of a reunited brotherhood of the
Jewish people was crumbling. The dark-skinned Jews from
Africa and Asia found themselves confined to ghetto-like
government housing that was little better than our Palestin-

ian villages and relegated to the poorest-paying jobs. Their anger was beginning to strain Israel to its political limits. And on religious issues, the Orthodox, the Reformed and the secularized Jews viciously attacked each other. The conservatives believed that the country's mounting woes were God's judgment against violence; the moderates and liberals accused the religious of "backwardness." Sadly, the country that was once hailed as Messianic could not heal its root problems.

And at the moment of my arrival, another more volatile issue was about to explode, making my presence in Jerusalem unwise if not outright dangerous. The long-straining tension between Israel and its Arab neighbors was about to rupture.

For nearly twenty years, Palestinian refugees had been trapped in teeming, poverty-burdened camps in Egypt, Lebanon, Syria and Jordan. Untrained in anything but agriculture, they were resented, viewed as a scab that had never healed into the complexion of their new societies. Such frustration had birthed the poorly-trained commando groups, whose night strikes across the borders brought only violent reprisals from the Israeli military.

The United Nations strenuously urged Israel to assume its responsibility for the plight of the refugees. Israel should offer a choice: allow the refugees to return to their villages and homes or pay them for the land that was seized. Similarly, West Germany had paid Israel millions in reparations fees since World War II, so the request seemed fair. Though the Israeli Premier, Levi Eshkol, wanted reconciliation, his opponents inside Israel—including the aging Ben Gurion—ranted furiously at his talk of a peace agreement with Arab nations. Negotiations dragged on fruitlessly throughout the spring of 1967. Threats grew harsh.

Suddenly, on May 22, Egypt blockaded the Gulf of Aqaba,

Israel's only water route for receiving oil shipments from the Persian Gulf. Gunships and mines halted tankers headed for Israeli ports, like a tourniquet cutting off Israel's vital energy supply. The roads from Jerusalem, Tel Aviv, Haifa and Tiberias were flooded with young men and women in khakis, with automatic weapons at their sides, all hitchhiking to join their reserve units. A strange fever—the loathing and the eagerness for war—was in the air.

The war, when it exploded, was actually won in a single day. Early on June 5, air raid sirens wailed through the city. Hours before, Israeli fighter planes had knifed through the skies of Egypt, Jordan, Syria and Iraq in a surprise attack, destroying nearly four hundred Arab jets as they sat wing-to-wing on their runways. The Sinai campaign and fighting in the Golan Heights lasted just a few more days, then it was over, leaving the world stunned in the wake of a "Six-Day War." For weeks Israel rode the crest of excitement, proclaiming a national holiday.

On the morning of celebration, I was still settling into my room in Jerusalem. The day before, I had given blood in a local hospital to aid Israeli soldiers wounded in the fighting. I was still feeling a little weak, but the sound of cheering drew me into the streets. Crowds swept me along the sidewalks to the Jaffa Road—to a sight that numbed me. Columns of soldiers, tanks, cannons and mortars were parading from the far suburb of Ramallah into Old City Jerusalem which had been captured from the Jordanians in bloody combat. Scanning the crowds, my breath caught painfully in my throat.

Hundreds of Christian ministers, priests and nuns cheered on the parade. One trio waved a banner that read: "Blessed is he that comes in the name of the Lord." Another banner said "Prophecy is fulfilled." All were smiling, applauding—hailing the machinery of war just as religious people had once cast palms before the Prince of Peace.

The scene blurred. Hot tears streaked my cheeks, and I struggled to push free of the crowd. I fled through the narrow streets of Old Jerusalem, searching for a quiet refuge. Instinctively, I found my way past the cluttered shops and slipped inside the massive doors of the Holy Sepulchre.

In the dim, looming church, I sank down on a bench. I felt betrayed. Alone. My difficult work at reconciling the Christians of Ibillin seemed so puny, so worthless in light of what I had just seen. I could understand the love of Christians for Jews—as my brothers I loved them too. But instead of demanding a true resolution to our conflict, my Christian brothers and sisters were applauding destructive might. And if Israel was so squarely in the center of prophecy and God's will, why was the nation coming unglued from within? The question of the suffering refugees was forgotten totally.

Numbly, I stared at the ornate sepulchre at the heart of the huge sanctuary. Surrounded by golden censers and candelabra, it was like a marble jewelbox. I thought of the words Jesus had spoken at His resurrection. Three times He said to His followers: "Peace be with you." And this risen Lord, who proclaimed the reconciliation of God and man, had also told them: "As my father sent me, I am sending you."

Was it more important to preserve these holy stones or to preserve peace between men, and human dignity? To insist and plead and struggle for it if need be? Who was going to become a beggar for peace if Christians did not?

After perhaps an hour, I rose to leave, with the pentrating sense that all my efforts were futile—my hopes and dreams dead. Dismally, the thought crossed my mind that in two days I was supposed to face Jewish students and professors at the Hebrew University. I wanted to hide—to lose myself back in Ibillin. For a moment, I thought of fleeing the country entirely. Perhaps the Jesus of my boyhood was not powerful enough to bridge the bitterest hostilities of men's hearts after all. Perhaps His idea of peace only extended to those who came to sit, quiet and contemplative, on a church bench.

As I walked from the church, heading for the dazzling summer sunlight outside, I noticed the words carved deeply in marble overhead. "He is not here. He is risen." Later, I would think back and realize that these words, etched in my memory, were strangely prophetic.

My reception at the university disarmed me totally.

On my first morning, I jostled my way nervously through the crowded corridors with my class registration papers in hand. At the first office a young, Jewish secretary took my forms, studied them, then looked at me questioningly.

"You are Elias Chacour?"

"Yes."

"You are Palestinian?"

At once I was wary. I could not escape the memory of interrogation at the port in Haifa two years before. If she asked me to step aside into a closed room, I was ready to dash down the hall and leave Jerusalem. "Yes," I said, "Palestinian."

She glanced down at my papers again, wrote several lines and handed them back. "Welcome," she said with a warm smile.

During my first semester I was continuously amazed at the graciousness of professors and scholars in each of my classes. I was welcomed and encouraged to express my viewpoint. These, I discovered, were men and women of intellectual integrity, moral and sincere. I had to admit that I was utterly surprised and I hoped it was more than superficial politeness.

One man who became an immediate close colleague was a Professor David Flusser. As it happened I was his only student one semester in a course on Greek Patrology. Flusser had a brilliant knowledge of this field, conversant in all the teachings and writings of the ancient Church fathers. More than anyone I was to meet, he seemed blind to the fact that I was Palestinian, probably because the wisdom of the ages had given him a pastoral sort of love for all people.

It was this love that drew us together into discussions that ranged far beyond course material. Since there were just two of us, our "class" usually convened in his modest apartment where archaeology, religion and politics were stirred together with endless cups of coffee. Slowly, gingerly, the Palestinian issue emerged, until one day toward the end of the semester, he thumped the table, startling me.

"God intended for the land of Israel to be a blessing for all nations—all people. Not just a few."

Delicately, I probed. "So you mean that? Really? For Palestinians, too?"

"Everyone," he insisted. "History dictates it. Not just our past, but our need for a peaceful future as well."

Walking home after our session, Flusser's words stuck with me. In a practical way, Israel's economy could not hold up for long with the tremendous expense that went for arms alone. And his comment about history stirred up memories of my research in Paris. I had concluded then that all Jewish people did not hate Palestinians. Many had been infuriated at the tough-minded government. This fact had seemed an important key, and now I knew it was true from my friendship with Flusser and others like him. I thought, *If only the whole nation of Israel—and the whole world—could understand that Jews and Palestinians can get along when they begin to treat each other with dignity.*

Though I was unaware, that prayer was already being answered in an unusual way. Since I was an oddity—a Palestinian scholar—I was soon invited to receptions and parties in some rarefied circles that included religious and govern-

ment leaders from Europe, Asia and America. Here I was
introduced to ambassadors, diplomats, influential ministers,
priests. I also met many leading rabbis from Jerusalem and
abroad who received me with apparent warmth. And I was
delighted that these powerful men wanted to discuss the
Palestinian crisis. As I talked, however, I could not help but
wonder whether their interest was purely superficial. They
seemed sympathetic, compassionate. Yet, it would be some
time before I felt the full impact of these frank discussions.

Not to say that everyone in Jerusalem politely accepted
my presence. Just when I felt that the thread of peace was
beginning to unite me with Jewish brothers such as Professor
Flusser, that thread would stretch to the breaking point
again.

In 1968, as my second year of studies progressed, Flusser
organized a special symposium for the scholars, in the Bible
Department, comparing the concept of love as expressed in
Judaism, Islam and Christianity. His real goal, he confided to
me, was to promote understanding between these groups
whose religious claims to the land of Israel kept them at each
other's throats like packs of dogs. And it was Flusser's opening remarks at the symposium that exposed some harbored
feelings.

Standing before his audience, Flusser began by saying,
"The Judaic concept of love is expressed in the conquest of
Jericho. Joshua destroyed the people of Jericho in the name
of God, because he loved his own people."

He commented briefly about Islam, then surprised us all
with the following statement: "Christian love is the seemingly impossible love. Something amazing to behold. It is the
love of the crucified who says, 'Father, forgive them for they
know not what they do.'"

At once a young scholar named Greenberg was on his feet

"You Flusser," he shouted, "you are a perverted Jew. You give the impression that Christianity is better than Jewry!"

There was a gulf of embarrassed silence. Flusser replied gently: "Not at all, Moshe. I'm just trying to tell you what I understand from my readings."

Greenberg persisted. "For me the love of Joshua is the only real love, because he dealt out retribution."

A chaos of voices arose, murmurs and angry shouts. I felt my face grow hot, and I gripped the arms of my chair.

In the din, another scholar rose. "Moshe," he said in a pleading voice, "it seems that your thinking would always lead to violence. You would always crush the opponent. With that kind of logic, what would you do with our Israeli Arabs?"

With an icy glance, Greenberg looked at him—then at me. "I would act accordingly." Around the hall, a dozen others murmured in agreement.

It was more than I could take. I fled from the hall with one of the deans at my heels. "Don't leave, Elias—please," he said, taking my arm. "We will change our discussion."

"I don't care about the discussion," I flared. "I want you to change the mentality!" I tried to pull my arm from him, but his grip tightened.

"Elias," his voice was commanding. "We *can* change the mentality. Are you giving up on us so quickly?"

Later, the dean's words needled me. I was not one to give up. I had expressed my views as openly as I dared, had worked hard among my own people. And I prayed daily for the reconciliation of Palestinians and Jews. What more was there?

As the fall semester of 1968 ground on, I grew fearful over Palestinian-Jewish tensions. After the 1967 war, the *fedayeen* groups that had been striking at Israel for some years were banding together under the name, Palestinian Liberation Organization. One man would arise to try to lead them—Yasser Arafat.

I grieved. Why had no Christian leader arisen to speak for my people?

And then I met Joseph Raya.

In October, I was summoned to meet the newly-elected Bishop of all Galilee. Several months earlier, our Patriarch had passed away and my Bishop had been elected to fill the vacant seat. I was more than mildly disappointed that this Raya, an American Lebanese from somewhere in the Southern U.S., had been chosen as my new Bishop.

When I was shown into his office, I began to bow in the greeting many bishops expected. But he stopped me. "I'm not here for that," he smiled. "Please sit down and tell me about all the people of Galilee."

And indeed he meant *all* the people—not just Melkite Christians. I began, of course, telling about my work in Ibillin. He paced the room as I spoke, watching me. The coiled vitality in his smallest movements made him seem much younger than his graying hair and middle-aged features indicated. If I paused, he would urge me on with probing questions: What about my relationship with the Jewish people? What was happening among the Moslems? The Druze? Was our Church helping the jobless? What were the conditions in Palestinian villages?

When I'd given everything I knew, I was out of breath Bishop Raya was still pacing vigorously. "And what do you think is the greatest need of all?"

"Hope," I replied. "Palestinians need the hope of a future Hope that one day we can reconcile with the Jews and live in dignity again."

He pondered this thought. It was then that I happened to

mention briefly the story of Biram and Ikrit and our efforts to rebuild the village church.

"That's it exactly," he sparked. "We'll stage a demonstration of our goodwill. "We'll rebuild the whole village of Biram."

I cringed at his naiveté. Politely, I explained that the only reason we had been allowed to touch the church was because of a government policy allowing the restoration of any religious site. I shook my head. "They won't let us lift a stone to rebuild the homes, I'm afraid."

His response nearly knocked me over. "They won't stop us," he said glowingly, "if we rebuild with living stones."

If I had thought Bishop Raya naive, I was far in the wrong. Before our conversation ended I learned the true story of this gentle firebrand of a man. His first assignment had taken him to Birmingham, Alabama, in 1950. Conditions among black Americans there had hardly changed since the days of slavery. There were still secret lynchings and open hatred. Despite threats and cold water hoses, a young, black minister named Martin Luther King, Jr., began to preach about his dream of equality and justice. Raya became one of King's fast friends, praying and marching at his side from Birmingham to Selma to Washington, D.C.

Now that same zeal, that sacrificial love for the outcast, was transplanted in Galilean soil. I was elated. My hopes, which had withered, caught his fire like dry kindling. Shortly after our meeting, we hit upon a plan: We would assemble fifteen hundred people for a peace gathering in Biram, representing the population of the village at the time of its destruction. Our goal was simply to show the government of Israel that Palestinians wanted only to return to their homes to live in peace. Bishop Raya began spreading the word through priests and village officials. And I, between finishing my last year-and-a-half of studies in Jerusalem, contacted uncles, cousins and other former villagers of Biram.

By the time I had completed my work in Jerusalem in 1970, we had refined our plan further: We would begin in August, staging a six-month camp-in on the ruins of Biram. I had moved back to Ibillin, resuming my pastoral duties, and was caught up in the final whirlwind arrangements for the camp-in. Many young people had begged to join our fifteen hundred enthusiastic supporters. So along with arranging for food and water, medical supplies and tents, I had to assure that a number of teachers would join us, since the demonstration would continue into the school year.

By August, I felt spent. Months of planning, meetings, phone calls and letter writing had drained me. For weeks, I had gotten by on three or four hours of sleep each night, despite the sisters' fussing that I needed to rest. Yet as I rode with a busload of volunteers from Ibillin to Biram, a certain electric tingle of excitement ran through me.

Bishop Raya had arrived in Biram before us, and was directing the first carloads of volunteers from the open square. When I stepped from the bus, I must have looked to him like the Apostle John just waking from his heavenly revelations. "Elias," he chuckled heartily, "come back down to earth. Your feet aren't even touching the ground."

He was right. I felt unearthly, as if I were living in a vision. The hot summer morning stretched into a cool evening, and I rushed about, helping volunteers to settle amid the fallen stones and timbers. The sky darkened, and still a vibrance drove me: voices mixed with laughter; women cooked over blazing wood fires; boys and girls played beneath the olive trees again. And still more busloads arrived, hundreds of Palestinian people coming, wave upon wave . . . and memory stirred me. . . .

. . . I was a young boy again, alone at the edge of the

Mediterranean with salt-spray dampening my face and waves crashing at my feet. Then, in a vivid waking dream, I had seen Biram come to life again—flooded with waves of people. . . .

And now, as a thin moon edged above the dark, eastern hills, I watched as my dream became a waking reality.

For six months, as fall slowly chilled the hill country, we worshiped, played, ate and slept in the open. The brisk rains drenched us, followed by cold winds that moaned through the cedars. From the very beginning, the news media sent photographers and reporters, keeping all Israel buzzing with news about our demonstration.

Though I never imagined it at the time, certain eyes had begun to watch us in secret—waiting for us to make one wrong step.

One frosty morning during the camp-in, Bishop Raya pulled me aside. Rubbing his hands before the glow of a fire, he said, "Elias, since God created us we've been kneeling to pray. For so long we've thought of prayer as hiding ourselves away to talk with God in private about our problems. But there's a time for setting aside our spiritual words and going out to our brother who has something against us. This is prayer, too—real intercession. It requires forgiveness and the strong love of God."

I knew there was some plan behind his words. Suspiciously, I asked, "What are you getting at?"

"It's good that we've rallied these people," he said, gesturing toward all the surrounding demonstrators. "It's a first step of hope for them. But the Jewish people need the hope of peace, too. It's time to march in Jerusalem and give our Jewish brothers the chance to walk at our side and show the world together that we are all against violence. That we all want human dignity."

Something caused me to recoil at his words. Was he mad?

Certainly his office had been deluged with hundreds of letters, phone calls and telegrams from Jewish rabbis and other Israeli citizens. We'd been told that more sacks of mail arrived each day, beleaguring the secretaries, and that the vast majority were in favor of a peaceful settlement between Jews and Palestinians. It appeared that the hearts of many Jews were indeed with us. But I could not believe that Jews would openly support us in a peace march.

He must have read my thoughts—or at least read the look on my face. Staring into the guttering flames, he said, "I'm not going to lie to you. This kind of intercession always involves a risk."

I took a deep breath of cold air and expelled a frosty sigh. "All right. We'll march together. You lead and I'll follow. At least they'll have two of us to arrest," I replied lightly.

"Oh no," said Raya with a sudden laugh. "You've missed the idea. I didn't say I would lead. I'll help organize and I'll march. But," he patted my shoulder, "a Palestinian must lead."

The march took almost eighteen months to organize. When the Biram demonstration ended, I returned to Ibillin and began writing letters to friends at the Hebrew University and to other Jewish acquaintances in Jerusalem. Their return letters were solidly supportive, but still left me with a deep foreboding—like the letter I received from a leading rabbi.

He was terribly dismayed, he said, at Golda Meir's notoriously tough stance toward Palestinians in Israel. With her "land reforms," she was confiscating more and more farmland from our villages. Shortly after coming to power, she had been asked by reporters how she planned to answer the Palestinian cry for justice. Her reply: "What is a Palestinian? Such a thing does not exist."[11]

My rabbi friend then wrote these astonishing words: "We

who seek God are terrified because your story is like that of Naboth and Jezebel. Among the rabbis, many I know are afraid that Golda Meir, like Jezebel, has 'sold herself to do evil' to your people."

My heart skipped. Further on, I read, "When you march, write on your placards: 'Golda Meir is killing justice—she is the modern Jezebel.' However," he hastily penned, "I would be obliged if you did not connect my name with that statement."

With a twinge of uneasiness, I dropped the letter on the stack of mail that covered my desk. All these letters and the gifts of money were wonderful. But what kind of support could we really hope for from our Jewish brothers when it came right down to marching in the streets of Jerusalem?

I had a sinking feeling. Several thousand Palestinian friends had pledged to march with us. Even Mother and Father were planning to come with a busload from Gish. As I thought of my parents—now in their seventies and showing the first tremors of frailty—and the other hopeful marchers, I shuddered, remembering the cold water hoses of Alabama, the police dogs and billyclubs . . . What if Bishop Raya and I were leading our people into a trap?

Early on the morning of August 13, 1972, our fleet of busses ground sluggishly up the steep roads to Jerusalem. Near the outskirts of the city, at a pre-arranged point on the Jaffa Road, we parked. We had chosen for our march the same route over which the victory parade of 1967 had gone. As I stepped off the bus, the sultry summer air engulfed me. The sun was already burning through the haze, but was not the only reason that perspiration streaked my temples.

Other busses pulled in from various regions. Marchers—all Palestinian so far—stepped out to stretch their legs and mix amiably with old friends and relatives from other vil-

lages. The jeep and megaphone we arranged for had arrived
But it was already 9:20—just forty minutes until the marcl
would begin. And I was still scanning the road toward Jerusa
lem for any sign of the Jewish friends who had promised t
march with us.

Bishop Raya tapped my shoulder. When I turned, he rea
my look immediately. "Trust, Elias," he said with a caln
smile. "We have risked. Now it's in God's hands."

More minutes passed. As I waited, Mother and Fathe
stepped from one of the late-arriving busses. Father cam
slowly down the steps, his white hair hidden beneath th
familiar *kafiyeh*. Mother followed. Her legs had weakened
but she still had a certain spunk in her step. We embraced
and I wished so deeply that they had stayed safely at home

"You're worried, Elias," said Father, his clear blue eye
studying mine.

Mother took my arm. "I've been worried for *you,* but onl
because you work too hard." I tried to ignore her con
ments—though it was true I had been plagued by fatigue-
and she persisted. "You do work too hard. But I didn't com
all this way to tell you that."

"Elias," Father continued, "You won't mind if we don
walk, will you? While you are out praying for peace in th
streets, we are going to stay here on the bus and talk
someone who is more important than anyone in the gover
ment. We will pray here."

I felt such warmth for them in that moment—and I w
thankful for their decision. But as they retreated to their bu
I was still plagued with doubt that our friends from Jerusale
would come.

In a few minutes, several cars pulled up, delivering abo
fifteen to twenty professors from the Hebrew Universit
With sinking hopes, I was about to greet them when I notice
other cars turning the corner onto Jaffa Road. More we

coming—in small groups. In a few more minutes, they were arriving on foot a dozen at a time. Among the growing crowd, more professors appeared, making a total of seventy supporters from the University. And at the same time others were arriving, groups of Moslems and Druze who had heard about the demonstration. And then my heart was racing.

Climbing nervously into the jeep, megaphone in hand, I hurriedly organized the marchers into lines. As I stood up before this sprawling crowd, the sight brought a lump to my throat. Near the jeep stood Bishop Raya, along with several priests and rabbis. Their heads were bowed, praying to the same God. A young Jewish man was handing out placards that read: "Justice for Biram and Ikrit," and "Justice for Palestinians." Further away, the marchers had already intermingled—Christian, Jew, Moslem and Druze. We had become one in this cause, ready to beg together for peace. And I noticed, too, as the driver started the jeep's engine, that a certain calm had come over me. My legs were no longer shaking as we moved slowly out onto Jaffa Road, the crowd surging behind us. Still I wondered—remembering all the volatile issues our presence represented—how we would be received.

As the march rolled block by block toward the heart of Jerusalem, it grew. At 10:00 a.m., the sidewalks were busing. Though stands of policemen had set protective cordons along our route, more and more people flooded our ranks. By the time we had reached our destination, the *Knesset*. I sensed the feeling of unity that ran like electricity through the marchers—now nearly eight thousand strong. The last shred of worry left, for it seemed that much of the city was behind us.

Surrounded by banks of cameras and friendly reporters, we congregated on the *Knesset's* wide, stone steps. The newsmen seemed amazed, snapping photo after photo of young Jewish men in *yarmulke* and older Palestinian men in *kafiyehs* sitting side by side. Here, Bishop Raya announced that he was requesting a formal meeting with Golda Meir to discuss reconciliation between Israel and the Palestinian people. If she would not see him, we would wait—as many as were able—to fast and pray.

Hundreds of us did wait—for four days as the blistering sun of August glared off the pavement, keeping prayer vigil by night or sleeping on the steps. Many, especially the elderly like Mother and Father, returned to the villages. And while I was deeply moved that we could pray and fast together for the peace of Jerusalem, the *Knesset* continued to present its closed, stone-silent face to us.

Bishop Raya's request to meet with Golda Meir was never answered. Though Jerusalem's police chief was quoted in newspapers as saying that ours was the most amazing demonstration of unity he had ever seen in Israel, the government ignored us. At the end of four days, when we called an end to our fast, I fought down disappointment.

As the crowd broke up, I walked dejectedly toward our bus. A university professor stopped me. "Elias, what's wrong? You're not pleased?" And before I could respond, he pointed back toward the *Knesset*. "Look there."

At the top of the steps was a large group of young men and women. By their varied dress, we could tell they were Christian, Jewish, Moslem and Druze. They stood with their arms around one another.

"You see, Elias," he announced. "Change is here. It's happening in people's hearts. Even if slowly. 'Righteousness and peace have kissed,'" he said, quoting a psalm. "And it was you who brought us together. You are a son of God."

We were nearly back to Ibillin. The rattling of the bus kept me awake as I stared out the window into the dark. Had something been accomplished? It was then that the inner voice—was it only memory?—reminded me of the professor's words. He, a Jew, had called me a "son of God." And that inner voice reminded me of a phrase I knew so well: *Happy are the peacemakers. . ."*

Walls were coming down.

# 12

## "Work, For the Night is Coming."

I lifted my head, listening, momentarily forgetting th mound of letters on the desk before me. Laughter rang fron the next room of the parish house where Ghislaine wa teaching a squirming bunch of kindergarten children. It wa just a few weeks after the march in Jerusalem and school wa well under way. Faintly, through the window beside my des in the back room, I could also hear Nazarena's choir practi ing in the church. Not long before, I had celebrated m thirty-second birthday and the children had eagerly ser naded me. Usually, these sounds made me smile—joyf sounds of what I had come to call "my love affair wi Ibillin." But this morning the singing and laughter did not all match my mood.

I slipped out to the garden, pacing up and down. Habit grapevine had grown thick and hearty, webbing its greene over a lattice of wooden poles. I fingered one of the coar leaves. Mère Macaire could make some savory grape le dishes—but she was gone. Age and hard work and our tou living conditions had eroded her already poor health. S had given six good years to Ibillin and, only weeks befor had passed away from us.

194

Her death, however, was not the only thing that stirred me as I strode between the new banks of flowers. A feeling of urgency tugged at me following our march for peace. A deskful of supportive letters from both Jews and Palestinians told me that a first bridge of reconciliation had been laid.

Yet I felt as though the stones had been set in place without mortar. Thousands and thousands of Palestinians were still struggling with basic survival—with poor housing and health care, no education, low-paying jobs or no jobs at all. Not surprisingly, they resented their position as the laboring class with no hope of raising themselves from the bottom of our society. If things did not begin to change for them, talk about reconciliation was wasted. How could I begin to get them across the bridge with me?

Several weeks later, when I visited Bishop Raya on some Church matters, he, too, seemed unsettled. He paced the office with his usual vitality, like a graying lion, but some underlying feeling clouded his face.

"Is something wrong?" I asked.

He looked directly at me, paused, and released a deep sigh. "Yes. Unfortunately, I had an angry visitor—from Rome."

Our march, it seemed, had gained international attention through the media. Immediately, one of our most powerful cardinals who lived in Rome had flown to Israel, descending upon Bishop Raya without warning.

"The Cardinal was angry—nearly raving," he said incredulously. "He demanded that I stay out of the streets and stick to Church affairs. What was worse, he said to me, 'What do you care about these damn Palestinians?'"

Bishop Raya, however, dismissed the affront with a wave of his hand. "It doesn't change a thing. I'm still here—and I'm not about to live in comfort, or like a mouse, while people are suffering.

"And," he shifted abruptly, "I shouldn't lay my burdens on you when something is obviously on your mind. You've been frowning since you walked in, Elias. What's the trouble?"

I shrugged. "The march is over. We had some good, brotherly feelings. What do we do now?"

He pursed his lips thoughtfully. "You once told me that Palestinians need hope. You've seen how many Jews are for you. There's hope in that. But you've got to continue to build up the Palestinians. They're like sheep without a shepherd."

"I know. And they need someone to unite them. They need to work for common goals. Our young people need the hope of a future. They must learn that they are worthwhile and productive citizens. If they don't gain self-respect they will always resent the Jews."

Bishop Raya nodded. "Exactly. When you build dignity you begin to destroy prejudice."

"That would be easy," I grumbled, "if our communities were already united. Or if we had good schools. But our children study in broken down buildings with outdated books."

"Elias," he said, with his innocent smile, "sometimes you must work and sweat if you are going to be a peacemaker. Not just talk and shout about it. *You* build the communities. *You* build the schools."

Driving back to Ibillin I was rankled. What was he suggesting—that I magically produce buildings, books and teachers out of thin air? With all the work on my hands, I firmly dismissed the notion.

It would be a full two years before the thought crossed my mind again. Besides my work in Ibillin, which had blossomed in my seven years there, I had thrown myself into another project shortly after my return from Jerusalem.

Other villages throughout Galilee had continued to ask that I send Christian women to live and work with them

Finally, I had chosen seven of the poorest villages and promised to see what I could do. With Bishop Raya's eager permission, I had arranged with Mother Josephate to send twenty-one young women from her community—three to each village—on short "Apostolic Holidays." They would teach hygiene, homemaking and use their minor skills in nursing, and they would teach the young people Scripture. With the enthusiasm Ghislaine and Nazarena had spread on their occasional returns to Nazareth, we had no trouble finding volunteers.

The love and goodwill these young women carried with them was contagious in the villages, too. Early in 1973, in fact, the village of My'ilia invited me to a gala celebration to honor the three sisters whom the villagers had quickly come to cherish. A small, makeshift platform stood at the center of the town, and crowds of men, boys and women with babies had already clustered around it when I arrived.

I sat beside the sisters and an array of local dignitaries, ready for the usual niceties and over-long speeches. Not to disappoint me, a stout little man, his suit vest nearly bursting its buttons as it stretched across his middle, rose and launched a rambling tribute. The young women at my side pinked with humility.

"Until the sisters came we had no one to care for us. Now we do not want them to leave. And so," he beamed at me, "we have collected a large sum of money as a gift for Abuna Chacour and the sisters—if they will stay."

The other dignitaries were nodding, but a warning sounded inside me. Allowing the sisters to stay would be no problem. From our conversations I knew their hearts had found a home here. But the money—it was like a scorpion I could not touch. Like other villagers, these people had long felt that the Church was too much in love with money. Yet, refusing a gift would violate our customs; it would be an insult.

The speaker was thrusting an envelope thick with money into my hands. Instead I jumped up and stepped to the podium.

"My friends, you are gracious—" I began delicately, "—too gracious. We cannot accept your money."

The crowd murmured uneasily. At once the little man beside me objected harshly: "It's a gift, Abuna. You cannot refuse—"

"But I do," I pressed. Something crucial was at stake here—the self-respect of this village. "Bread and olives are enough for these young women. They have come here as servants. They see God in your faces.

"And this," I said emphatically, snatching the envelope and waving it in the air, "does not repay them. Giving money to the Church cannot fulfill your obligation of love. You must give more than that. You must be willing to serve, too."

Even as I spoke, Bishop Raya's thoughts on building came back to me, igniting a plan in my head. I rushed on.

"The gift we *will* accept is a commitment of service. You too must give your hands and your backs to work—not for us but for your children. This money will be used to start a library where your children will sharpen their minds. And there is more."

I could see by the dawning smiles that the crowd was suddenly with me. "We are going to build a community center—a place of learning and friendship for the whole village. Will you help? Will you give your time, your hands and back? I am willing to give mine, but I cannot build alone."

The challenge caught like fire, and the crowd burst into applause.

Immediately, the whole band of dignitaries rose and embraced me, their honor intact. "We will give our hands *and* our money," my little friend announced proudly.

The sisters happily remained. The front room of their small home was soon stacked from floor to ceiling with shelves of new and used library books.

And over the next two years, men, women and young people gladly sacrificed hours of free time to build their community center. Three or four times a week, I would return to My'ilia to help and supervise. And with each layer of blocks, I could feel the dignity of the village strengthening.

One disturbing event marred the excitement. Late on a summer night, some men were returning home through the dark streets when they heard loud crashes coming from the nearly completed building. They sprinted up to the open doorway in time to see two or three figures slip away through the blackness, down the street and out of My'ilia—and they found windows shattered, buckets of paint dumped.

We never did catch the vandals, but the question nagged: Who were they? To prevent further incidents, we stationed night watchmen in the center. And construction went on.

For me, the *real* work was still ahead. In these centers, I planned to have lecture series and films to promote village unity. More than physical buildings, I wanted to construct a bridge of understanding about our Jewish brothers.

Before I could pursue these further plans still another challenge opened before me.

Evidently, some of the Church leaders I had met at the Hebrew University had carried back to their home countries reports of a certain Palestinian Christian whose words had some spark. While the building in My'ilia rose slowly, I received several invitations from churches in Holland and Germany that wanted to hear my ideas about peace. Still I puzzled as I drove to the airport: What could I, an unknown priest from the poor parishes of Galilee, have to say to sophisticated Europeans?

At the bustling airport in Germany, Lony and Franz threw their arms around me. In the nine years since I had last seen them, Wolfgang had grown into a tall fourteen-year-old who gripped my hand tightly, and two lovely daughters had been born, Rita Maria and Michelene.

After exchanging pleasantries, Wolfgang surprised me. With a look that seemed too intense and searching for an adolescent, he asked, "Have you heard about the nuclear arms race?"

Franz, who was loading my bag into the car, shook his head. "Who is going to bring the world back to sanity Elias?" And as we drove away from the airport toward home he told me about the contagion of fear, like a plague from the Dark Ages, that was over-shadowing Europe: It's name was *nuclear holocaust*.

I knew, of course, that the United States and allied powers were locating nuclear-tipped missiles throughout Europe weapons of death that were aimed at Russia. The Russians made no secret of the fact that their own missiles were aimed both at the U.S. and the European bases as well. Lony and Franz now informed me of the strangling despair among the young people of Europe. "Many of them feel there is no answer—no hope."

As I kept my engagements, with these words in my head, knew I was addressing sophisticated men, women and young people who were jaded by political rhetoric, opportunism and broken promises. Yet, standing before each crowd, could only begin with the words that had long captivated me: "Blessed are the peacemakers. . . ."

Not that I was simplistic; nor was I easy on them. I told them the way of a peacemaker was difficult—it required deep forgiveness, risking the friendship of your enemies, begging for peace on your knees and in the streets. My audience seemed rivetted when I talked about the schools and conmunity centers I hoped to build throughout Galilee in an attempt to restore the dignity of my people.

The response surpassed my most far-flung expectations. Church leaders, for their part, amazed me with pledges of financial support for construction. The young people astounded me more: On the spot, many of them volunteered their time and labor to help the Galilean villagers. I was grateful beyond words. And before I left Germany, churches were planning to organize and send out these volunteers as soon as possible.

And in Holland, the response was even more overwhelming. Wherever I traveled throughout the green, canal-veined countryside, I met a simple, plain-spoken people who were also hungry for words of peace. And they were eager for a true report about the Palestinian people.

Through a friend, I was introduced to Cardinal Alfrink, a leader in the growing, international peace movement called *Pax Christi*. The Cardinal, in turn, surprised me by arranging a meeting with Princess Beatrix, soon to be Queen of Holland, in her stately and flower-trimmed residence in The Hague. At this stunning reception, I was moved to tears when the Prime Minister presented me with a huge bouquet of roses—one for each year of the Palestinians' exile.

As I returned to Ibillin, I rode on a cloud of excitement. The German churches had promised finances and young workers; the Dutch churches had promised volunteers also. The Reformed Church of Holland and the powerful Inter-Church Coordinating Committee had pledged their strong financial support. A television producer had even cornered me to plan a documentary—"One Day of My Life in Galilee"—for Dutch national television.

However, when Nazarena and Ghislaine greeted me, frowning with worry over my travel-weary appearance, I realized that my excitement was for something else: A tre-

mendous and growing group of people were becoming true
intercessors for peace—not just for the preservation of their
own countries, but for the future of the whole world. I was
not alone.

The trip to Europe was a bright spot amid the growing
tension in and around Israel. For several years the Middle
East suffered many swift blows against any peace efforts.
The most horrible were the murders of eleven Israeli athletes
by a radical group of *fedayeen* at the Munich Olympics, and
the 1973 Yom Kippur war—the third major Middle East war
in twenty-five years. The PLO, which had been driven from
Jordan by King Hussein, had settled in peaceful Lebanon
from which it masterminded raids and the hijacking of air-
liners. The Israeli government, still fighting the symptoms
without doctoring the real disease, quietly launched an ag-
gressive plan in reprisal: first, to crush the PLO out of
Lebanon at all costs; and second, to tighten its hold on
Palestinians within Israel.

However, I tried to ignore the government sanctions
against us—the land "reforms" that took away more and
more arable land from Palestinian villages, the unwarranted
week-long curfews particularly in the West Bank and Gaza at
crucial times in the planting or harvesting of crops. In a time
of private meditation, another of Jesus' sayings gripped me
with force: *Work . . . for the night is coming. . . .* And I
would work.

In the summer of 1974, I threw my energies into building
another community center in the village of Fassutah. Some
of the first young Europeans had arrived for a summer of
volunteer work, and with them the promised finances, so we
began construction at once.

I had driven to Fassutah one morning to deliver letters
from Europe to several of the volunteers when a bank of

village boys swarmed my car. "We talked to your friends last night, Abuna," one of them shouted, leaning inside the car window. "There were two of them and they asked a lot of questions—all about you and the center. They wanted to know what it was going to be used for. . . ."

He jabbered on, and I felt an uneasy curiosity about these men who called themselves "friends." The only description the boys could give me was so vague it could have been almost any two men in the country.

Since these phantom friends did not return, I brushed the incident aside. What captured my total attention was the amazing transformation in the people of Fassutah—just as it had occurred in My'ilia. As the center rose, the leaders were already planning bigger things: a library and eventually a school. Bishop Raya's instincts had been correct. With a little help and a common goal, the bent backs of these people were straightening. By working together they were building more than walls and windows, they were restoring the dignity that was a first step toward becoming first-class citizens again.

The following year began with the same running excitement that had carried me since my trip to Europe. With my work intensifying, and with more volunteers soon to arrive, I was fortunate that several men had become stalwarts in the church in Ibillin. Abu Mouhib, for one, was no longer the crusty policeman who used to swagger the streets, but a trusted brother. And though I was still leading services and was involved in community decisions, I had to trust to their wise judgment on some matters while I was busy in other villages. For in 1975, the cry came from Gish.

Gish was so remote that, unlike the more southerly villages which had some limited school facilities, it had few if any teachers to call upon and nothing but the most delapidated textbooks. They desperately needed a school. Since

Mother and Father had been living in Gish for the full twenty-eight years of our exile from Biram, acting as loving grandparents to many of the children, I expected great support and an easy time.

But not so. The first problem began when Bishop Raya telephoned to say that he urgently needed to see me. When I arrived in his office, his face was ashen.

"I'll tell you straight, Elias. The Church has reassigned me. I'll be leaving for Canada very shortly."

I felt wounded. Reassignment is not uncommon for clergy in many churches. But in Bishop Raya's case I felt that the reasons were all wrong. Recently, he had sold a few of the Church's many land holdings to poor farmers at a very, very low cost. It seemed obvious to me that the hierarchy was distraught at the loss of their *terra sancta*, as well as Bishop Raya's outspokenness. And so they were removing him.

"Don't be upset," he said, his expression lightening. "It's not the Lord you're losing. And others are behind you—others who see our goals."

In a few weeks he was gone. Despite his assurances, things began to sour.

The new Bishop, it appeared, was bothered about projects and building plans over which he had no control. And somehow a dispute arose over the fact that Moslems were helping with the construction of the school in Gish and that Moslem children would be allowed to attend. Though I was disturbed, I offered to step out of the project entirely, trusting the people of Gish to make the right decisions. I certainly needed a rest. The people would not hear of it though, and it was also at their insistence that the Bishop finally gave his blessing.

What shook me most was a near-fatal "accident."

That summer, seven German boys had come to Gish to work on St. Chrysostom Academy, for that was what we had christened this, our first new school. Construction was moving rapidly—and then our phantom "friends" made their presence felt again.

Since Gish was so far from Ibillin, I made fewer excursions to the site each week. Early one morning in August, however, an urgent phone call summoned me—something about trouble at the school. I hung up impatiently, for I had pressing matters in Ibillin that day, and sped off—a little too recklessly—toward the upper Galilee.

A group of young men, German and Palestinian, were gathered outside the shell of the school when I sped into Gish. In their paint-spattered work clothes and boots, they nearly dragged me from the car.

"Abuna," said one German boy, "we had prowlers last night. We heard some noises, but when we got here we saw no one. Then this morning we found these." He pointed to the ground.

It had rained during the night, and the churned muddy earth was pocked with fresh footprints all around the building, leading inside.

"We haven't checked to see if anything was stolen or destroyed, but we decided to call you—"

I was not listening. I was angry. Angry about similar annoying incidents at the previous building sites. All seemed calculated to induce fear. What did these prowlers want? Were they, in fact, the same men who seemed to be stalking me from village to village? *Who* were they? And I was angry at myself for forgetting to post a watchman.

Like a charging bull, I stomped through the mud to inspect for damage. Gripping the main support of a huge scaffold, I swung myself underneath to get inside the building.

"Abuna! *No!*"

I jerked around to look at the boys who had seen—too late—that the support had been forced out of its mooring. And in that second, huge planks loaded with bricks and mortar pails thundered down at me. A sickening *crack* stung my head, and I was pitched down into the mud—away from the collapsing scaffold.

In a haze of pain I lay gasping for air. The boys were around me—distantly—shouting my name. As my eyes cleared, I reached up with dirt-covered fingers and gingerly touched my throbbing head. My hand came down soaked with red, and suddenly my eyes were stinging. I felt faint.

The boys lifted me to my feet. Once I had steadied, I refused their offer to go for medical help. Instead, pressing a cloth to my wound with one hand, I drove myself to a doctor nearby, where it took more than two dozen stitches to close the gash. I felt foolish at my own charging carelessness and angry at the men, whoever they were, who were trying to scare me. However, I would not give up.

Perhaps I might have recognized in all this the taming hand that seemed to be trying to slow me. I would do it my own way though, with dogged determination. And I hardly noticed that the inner quality that gave me stability—the very quality I was trying to teach my people—was dangerously strained. Even the completion of a comfortable apartment for me above the old parish house did not induce me to relax. Nazarena would peer at me with her dark, caring eyes, and Ghislaine would shake her head in a grandmotherly way, for they could see that I was becoming a brusque, snappish, driven man.

By the time the school in Gish was finished two years later, I was deeply engrossed in three major activities.

The first was the construction of a Peace Center in Ibillin.

In 1977, as we laid its foundations, the world was thrilling at the possibility for peace in the Middle East as Egypt's President Anwar Sadat made his famous pilgrimage to Jerusalem. Throngs of Israelis greeted him, cheering, weeping, hungry for peace after years of fighting. But peace was a long way off. Before Sadat's arrival, Prime Minister Begin told the press that Sadat would ask for a solution to the Palestinian problem and that anything but the present arrangement was impossible. Two years later, when the two leaders would sign the much-applauded Camp David peace treaty, their "solution" for Palestinians was so ambiguous it would prove useless.

As Jerusalem prepared to raise Egyptian flags to welcome Sadat, I knew that political agreements could not change hearts. My work in the community centers was all the more urgent if reconciliation was ever to come. In fact, I inaugurated each center by showing the film, *The Diary of Anne Frank,* so that Palestinian young people could understand the horrors Jews had suffered under the Nazis and forgive. And it was a warning against turning to violence. Always there were tears, for the story could well have been that of many Palestinian girls as well.

The second project was a youth camp. Since my years in Paris, I had often winced at the deprivation of Palestinian youngsters. For the boys there was only the endless game of soccer. And for girls, who were obliged to help in the home, there were few opportunities for recreation. So I had invited young people in several villages to camp beneath the olive trees of Ibillin for three weeks of sports activities, trips to the Mediterranean and teachings in the Scriptures. To my great joy, the five hundred young people we expected turned into a swarm of eleven hundred boys and girls. Each one was, to me, another living stone in the great bridge of understanding I wanted to build.

And thirdly, since my first speaking engagements in Europe, invitations had continued to come. I saw each one as a crucial opportunity to teach the Beatitudes, to proclaim the message of peace and to tell the outside world about our life in Galilee. I made several trips, first throughout continental

Europe where the Dutch television special and a few magazine articles about my work had drawn much favorable attention. In several countries there, and later in Ireland, I
marched with groups for the *Pax Christi* movement, raising
my voice with theirs against the threat of nuclear destruction
and militarism. On another occasion I was invited to India
where I read the words of Jesus, not only to Christians, but to
several thousand Hindus.

My travels would eventually take me to America and
Canada. Though I would have the privilege of speaking at
Harvard University, to me, the greatest support in these
countries came from many rabbis who invited me to speak to
their congregations. In Washington, D.C., for example, I
was a guest in the home of Rabbi Eugene Lipman of the
Temple Sinai, and in Chicago, I spoke to a large group at the
K.A.M. Isaiah Israel Congregation led by Rabbi Arnold
Jacob Wolf. I was pleased and grateful when many of these
rabbis sent me off, not only with their prayers but with gifts
of money for my work.

Like a parched man squeezing drops from a waterskin, I
drew encouragement from this outside support. Throughout
the Middle East, the political situation was swaying, and I
had begun to feel that I was teetering between hope and fear.

Real trouble was brooding just across the border in Lebanon. In 1978, in the wake of a two-year civil war, Lebanon's
so-called Christian Militia was still struggling against the
Moslems. The PLO had taken opportunity during the turmoil to entrench itself further, and now the Syrians were
intervening against the PLO. I sensed a deeper trouble, too,
for Israel was planning to send in "peacekeeping forces,"
which alarmed me. It alarmed large numbers of Jewish Israelis, too, for peace seemed so close, and popular anti-war

groups like Peace Now, Courage and Peace and others were protesting military involvement.

As the world watched our teetering scales of peace and war, the direction of my life tipped drastically.

In January 1980, I was again planning a special project for our young people. In three years the summer camps had burgeoned to include nearly four thousand from Akko on the coast to far Gish. My greatest hopes were pinned on these boys and girls, for from them I received the greatest rewards. One group of Moslem children, for instance, had presented me at the end of one camp with an inscribed tray. It said: "Thank you, Abuna. You have taught us how to love Christ."

But summer was still months away, and I had another exciting plan.

Whenever I worked with our young people, they prodded me—with an endless fascination—to tell about Biram and Ikrit which had become legendary. As I described our past, Father's prayers, Mother's stories, the rhythm of an easier time, I longed—deeply longed—for a place of quiet and rest, for my life had become such a whirlwind. To my delight my young friends listened, their faces intent with a wistful longing for such a place, too. I saw in these yearnings, a chance to usher them across the bridge of reconciliation with me.

On a crisp morning one month later, I was marching up the steep road to Biram. It was February 23, a special day for planting trees in Israel. Pacing along behind me were nearly four hundred Palestinian boys and girls, each excitedly bearing an olive sapling. We were going to plant our trees amid the ruins as a sign of peace to the government. I had sent special invitations to members of the *Knesset,* and I hoped that at least a few of them would come.

We climbed the sloping road, between groves of trees,

with white and gray clouds scudding across a cold blue sky, and my spirit quickened. I was going to show these young friends *my* Biram. The church, now fully restored, had been painted the previous summer by several of the German boys, and I had brought in a new bell to hang in its tower. I would ring the bell after . . . then my heart skipped.

Rounding a sharp bend, I saw in the road ahead a barricade of barbed-wire and a dozen jeeps. Behind the wire, their guns braced across their chests, were soldiers.

Behind me, the marching footsteps stopped uncertainly, but I did not look back. I kept on marching, my small olive tree held out in the open, right up to the barricade.

"Let us through. We have come with olive branches, not guns."

From behind his barricade, the commanding officer replied stiffly, "Go away. We have orders not to let you pass."

"Why?" I demanded.

"Those are the orders. You don't need any other reason."

Farther up the hill, where the road wound past Biram and on toward Lebanon, I could hear the growl of truck motors. What were they doing?

"We have come for peace," I said as calmly as I could. "What have *you* come here for?"

His eyes were unwavering. "I'm afraid that's not your business. Now leave."

When I turned, hundreds of other eyes met me. A moment before, they had been bright with hope. Now the light had gone out.

Later that night, I sat alone in my apartment. In front of me was a copy of the letter I had sent to the Speaker of the *Knesset,* Yitzhak Shamir, along with a surprise gift of almost four hundred olive trees. And in my mind's eye were the unforgettable faces of the young marchers. I had led them to a bridge and we could not get across. Could we ever?

*And what does it matter?* The thought surprised me. I knew it had been creeping around the edges of my conscious mind for months. I tried to fight it, listing the accomplishments—schools, libraries, community centers, the caring friends around the world. Somehow it was not enough.

I was forty years old, and feeling every bit of it just then. I had prayed and worked for something for more than thirty years. I was exhausted—and suddenly willing to be finished with it all. The sense that my moves were being watched had become too much.

Wearily, I rose from my chair, switched off the light and went to bed. It would take a good deal of time, perhaps, but I could begin a new life for myself.

# Chapter 13

## One Link

The morning sun was already blistering and I had a headache. It was July 1981. I was again walking on a hillside near Biram. This time I had come bearing, not an olive tree, but a casket.

Mother was dead. She had slipped from us peacefully in her sleep.

Age had eventually forced Mother and Father to move from Gish to Haifa to be near my sister and brothers. Mother's last wish was to be buried in Biram. It grieved me that she had died so far from the home she had longed for until the end. Atallah, Musah, Rudah and I set her casket beside the tomb, then took our place beside Father, Wardi and a hundred tearful relatives and friends.

Inadvertently, my hand slipped into my pocket and found the precious memento Mother had given me. Had she known death was so near when she parted with this small treasure? I fingered the familiar shapes—the doves and fish of her beloved necklace. One day she had surprised me by slipping it off and placing it in my hand. "Be strong, Elias," she had said. "What you do matters. Especially for the young ones."

"Grant her rest, O Lord . . . ."

*Rest.* I stared off over the heads of the mourners as the priest intoned, stared at the rising mountains and beyond them to Lebanon. When I had last come to this place more than a year before, I had concluded that there was no rest for us in this life. It was not just the aborted march with the olive trees that had convinced me. I was remembering a recent incident far more terrifying. . . .

I had been summoned by the Patriarch on Church business, and was traveling through Lebanon. Unknown to me, as I displayed my papers at the border, some unseen watcher was making a phone call.

Hurriedly, I caught a taxi and headed north toward Beirut. The driver launched a monologue that rambled on about recent skirmishes and the hardships his family was suffering in Lebanon's political turmoil. I listened politely, and in a while the jagged skyline of Beirut rose in the distance.

Just at the outskirts of the city, we stopped at a red light. I leaned forward to give the driver further directions—when suddenly the rear door next to me jerked open.

"Get out!" A man in dark clothing was shouting, pointing an automatic rifle just inches from my face. "Quickly. Or I'll shoot."

Another gunman stood at the driver's window, a weapon trained on the poor man. "You say nothing," he growled. "If you report this, we'll find you. We have your license number."

Reflexively, I grabbed my suitcase, and the two men shoved me into the back seat of an old car that had stopped beside us at the light. The men slid in on either side of me and the driver slammed down on the accelerator, squealing tires on pavement.

"Who are you?" I demanded. I wanted desperately to sound brave, but my voice quavered. "Where are you taking me?"

"Shut up," growled the man who had dragged me from the taxi.

"Just tell me what you want with me. I'm no criminal. I'm here on Church business—"

"*Shut up!*" he roared, his unshaven face red with anger. He cursed me furiously, and I dared not speak again.

For nearly an hour we drove around the outskirts of the city. If they were trying to confuse me as to my whereabouts, there was no need. I was too shaken to notice anything but the guns still cocked and ready.

Near West Beirut, they turned abruptly onto a rubble-strewn street amid decaying buildings. Men and women sat idly on steps as we sped by. And suddenly I realized that this place—more decrepit than any big city ghetto I had ever seen—was one of the refugee camps. Why were they taking me there?

We stopped before a two-story building on a deserted street and they dragged me from the car. "You won't be needing this," grunted one of the men, wrenching my suitcase from me.

Up a flight of stairs we marched, a gun muzzle stuck uncomfortably in my back. In a panic, I thought, *They're going to murder me and no one will ever know.*

Instead, they shoved me into a room that was no more than a cement cubicle. They did not enter, but slammed the door behind me. In the middle of the room was a table with one chair on either side. Trembling, I sat down, resting my forehead on the table.

In a moment, I tried to pray, and the only words that came to mind were from Psalm 33: *The eye of the Lord is upon them that fear him, upon them that hope in his mercy—to deliver their soul from death. . . .* I repeated these words of comfort as the minutes passed. I had no certainty that m kidnappers would not murder me and fling my body in some vacant building. But a quietness of spirit came over me.

After nearly half an hour, the door burst open. I looked up to see a short, handsome young man swagger in with the two gunmen following. On the young man's hip I spotted a pistol. He sauntered over and sat in the chair opposite me, staring with fathomless eyes.

He kept staring and finally asked with a cold directness. "What's your business in Lebanon?"

"I'm a Melkite," I responded. "I was on my way to see the Patriarch when your men—"

"The *truth!*" he shouted, startling me. "I want the truth. You call yourself Chacour, but who are you really?"

That he knew my name surprised and scared me. I realized then that this bantam of a man was not an ordinary thug, but part of an organization. He had power.

For the next forty-five minutes he alternately coaxed and bullied me, sometimes impatient to the point of fury. I could not understand why he was asking me questions on military matters, and said so. The gunmen at the door were getting restless. Strangely, the calm did not leave me. In fact, I got bold enough to challenge him.

"Look," I faced him squarely. "I am Elias Chacour. I have cousins in a camp near here. We were driven out of northern Galilee. My family lived in Biram where—"

"From Biram?" he asked, suspiciously. "If that's so, tell me about it. Who did you know there?"

Gladly, I named the village *mukhtars* and a dozen families. I described the coming of the soldiers. When I began to tell about my current work in the villages, the schools and community centers he stopped me.

"That's enough," he said quietly. "I believe you." He motioned to the men to put down their guns. "Please accept our apologies, Abuna, for scaring you. If you want to come and sit in my chair, I'll answer any of your questions."

Without hesitation I fired, "Who are you?"

With a respect as great as his former belligerence, he replied, "I'm a commander in the PLO, and you must understand that we are very much afraid for our women and children."

"Is that why you kidnap?"

"Please, Abuna. Let me finish," he pursued. "Our intelligence had learned that some three hundred infiltrators have been coming into Lebanon. They have orders to burn churches and mosques so that Christians and Moslems will turn against each other. But we know there is another purpose. Once Lebanon is in turmoil, they will sweep through and kill us—and not us only, but our wives and our babies, too."

I listened, still too rattled to comprehend this supposed plot he was revealing to me.

"And so we followed you from the moment you entered the country. I had to have my men pick you up for questioning."

"And if I had not mentioned Biram, what then? Who would have known that you brought me here—or what you did with me?"

"No one," he replied levelly. "No one at all."

Suddenly I was too eager to be free of that desolate room— away from these desperate-sounding men—to ask more questions. I asked if I might leave, and they politely ushered me outside to the car. The commander asked, "Where can we take you, Abuna?"

"Just leave me outside this camp," I said, trying not to sound too eager. "I can find my way somehow."

As we drove toward the outskirts of the camp, I noticed a group of small boys playing ball amid the litter. They were laughing and shouting, lost in youthful abandon. Despite their shabby clothing, they might have been the children of any other country in the world.

When at last the car pulled up to a curb at the far end of the street, I hoisted out my suitcase. Even if I had to walk a ways I suspected I could soon catch another taxi.

"By the way," I said, turning to the driver, "what do they call this place?"

"It's called Sabra," he replied.

Mother's funeral was over. Wardi helped Father into a waiting automobile, hurrying him out of the sun's heat, and I climbed in next to him. We wound our way down the hills as I drank in the beauty of the cedar groves, the streams that still cascaded even in the dead of summer. Beside me, Father looked regal even in his loss. I had not told him, nor anyone else, about my decision yet.

Many times the face of my kidnappers had come to me. Then, as now, I had concluded that this "plot" to kill them sounded far-fetched, like the paranoid hauntings of violent men. Still the kidnapping had been a large factor clinching my decision. It had taken some time to disentangle myself enough from work in the villages and the church in Ibillin, but I was ready. I glanced at Father. Wardi and my brothers would take good care of him. And I would visit from time to time. Visit, but not stay.

On previous trips to Europe I had been offered a teaching position at a prestigious, Christian university. My superiors would certainly have approved such a move, but then I had declined. Now, I convinced myself, I deserved a rest. More than that, I could most likely do more good for the Palestinian people by educating others to our situation. And after all, hadn't my travels brought in so much support in prayers and money over the years? And what more could I do here?

I would be leaving Israel.

It was a pleasant morning in September 1982, and I was traveling in West Germany, speaking again in various churches. That day in particular, I would be speaking to a group in Böblingen, a lovely town near Stuttgart. I rushed about the room, rummaging through my suitcase and muttering about all the things I had forgotten. Nazarena and Ghislaine had just nodded somberly when I had told them I would be sending for more of my things when I was settled. Then I would write to the Bishop.

But somehow, I was finding it hard to settle into the new life I so wanted. A few offers had come my way. I had even opened my mouth to accept one—but something inside had stayed me.

Not that my mind had changed. Two months earlier, in July, Israel had invaded Lebanon on a "peacekeeping mission," though many Israeli soldiers had accepted prison sentences rather than fight in what they felt was an unnecessary war.

So I had stubbornly set my face like flint to find my new life in Europe. Perhaps, I thought as I hurriedly drove to the church in Böblingen, I'll find what I'm after on this trip.

At the church, I began my usual talk on the Sermon on the Mount. As I went through the lessons I had learned about being a peacemaker, however, I felt a certain flatness about my words. In the audience, several people yawned and a man in the very front pew kept checking his watch. At the back, I noticed that a friend of mine, a woman I knew from previous visits to West Germany, had slipped in late. But, trying to push on with my faltering message, I did not catch her pained expression.

"And," I insisted, hammering home my points about reconciliation, "it does no good for you to sympathize with me as a Palestinian if it means that you hate the Jewish people as a result. That's not what I'm here for. We, all of us, have to become the preserving salt of the earth. Do you agree?" I asked, leaning into the microphone.

Many were nodding, but my friend in the back surprised me by jumping to her feet. It was then I saw her tears.

"Abuna," she said, her voice cracking, "You have not heard the news?"

"No, what news?"

"In Lebanon, near Beirut, they have massacred hundreds of Palestinian refugees. Men, women, babies. In two camps—called Sabra and Shatila."

I was aware that all eyes were upon me. Inwardly I felt only hazy, roiling emotions through the numbness. I could not go on speaking, but closed with a brief, stumbling prayer. As I hurried out of the church I scarcely heard the words of condolence.

"We are so sorry for your people."

"A tragedy."

One young man was shaking his head, with a look of such utter desolation. "Senseless. It's all senseless."

In my room I sat rivetted to the television as newsmen confirmed the horrifying tragedy in more vivid detail throughout the day. Scenes of buildings blown to rubble flashed on the screen, and splayed bodies. The announcers said that the death toll was climbing. Lebanon's own Christian Militia had swept into the camps, ostensibly to drive out the PLO. They had been allowed into the settlements by Israeli defense forces which had dismissed the multi-national peacekeeping troops, promising to protect the unarmed refugees. Instead the militiamen had machine-gunned everyone in sight—mothers with babies in arms, teenagers, old men and women too feeble to flee—and bulldozed many of the bodies into mass graves.

And, the reports continued, European sources in the Middle East had confirmed that Israeli troops had sealed off the

two camps just before the massacre, warding off newsmen
with the assurance that they were just "protecting" the
camps despite the sounds of gunfire coming from within.

The Israeli government would balk at a worldwide outcry
for a complete investigation. Only after Israeli citizens insisted, outraged at the massacre, would Prime Minister Begin concede. And the world would know the truth: Though
Israeli soldiers had not actually killed the people of Sabra
and Shatila, they had known it was planned and stood guard
outside the camps while innocents met their death.

All over the world, reporters interviewed citizens who
were shocked and saddened by the tragedy. Most moving
were the scenes from Jerusalem where thousands of mourners—Jews and Palestinians together—had gathered in the
streets, weeping and bearing candles.

One woman so poignantly expressed the anguish of the
crowds amassing outside the *Knesset*. "I was awake all night
crying and despairing," she said, her face a mask of pain.
"What will become of us? What is happening to us?"

When I could watch no longer, I switched off the set and
fell back on the bed. Before me was the face of the young
PLO commander who had told me of his desperation. Was he
among the dead? I remembered the bank of boys playing ball
in the street. Were they buried in the rubble now?

*Senseless . . . senseless . . .* The words of the young man
at the church in Böblingen tormented me. Certainly the
killing was senseless, but not the lives that were lost.

Then I was remembering another band of small boys who
were playing soccer in a sand lot years before. I was among
them. I had found the arm buried in the sand. But I had lived.
Was that, too, senseless? An accident? Chance? Or was
there some reason that I had been spared?

Then I spotted it, lying in the suitcase I had flung open
haphazardly that morning. Mother's necklace. It was the

only memento from home I had packed. I rolled over, and the
doves and fish jingled brightly as I lifted it.

With the sound, Mother's voice returned to me. *Be strong,
Elias. What you do matters. Especially for the young ones.*

Now, suddenly, her words burned within me—burned with
consuming force. If I simply allowed time to sift its dust over
these latest deaths, I would be like those who had ignored the
sufferings of the Jews for centuries, or like those who had
turned their backs on my own people. Like those others, I
had been trying to find the easy life of blindness to pain.

These thoughts sparked another memory, from the writings of the Apostle Paul to his friends in Colosse: *And now I
am happy about my sufferings for you, for by them I am
helping to complete what remains of Christ's sufferings on
behalf of his body. . . .*" Here was mystery, a deep treasure
of the faith that I had not understood before. Now I saw that
Paul had given his hands and feet and tongue, his whole
body, to carry on the work of Christ after His death—even if
it meant the work of suffering.

Was I willing to go back, if it meant more hardship, living in
the midst of violence—possibly death? Could I, by continuing the long, slow labor of teaching young people the treasures of the Sermon on the Mount, point them toward true
peace? I was not sure, but I could only think of the faces I had
just seen on the television—people young and old around the
globe, weeping, linked by their yearning for peace.

That inner calm pressed in on me again, as I had not felt it
for a long, long time—a calm that seemed to come from a
familiar, taming hand.

I looked at Mother's necklace curled neatly in my palm.
Each link was beaten and hand-fitted by some skilled crafts-
man. I had not fully known about peace before. It was not at
all like a slim thread, as I had thought. Peace was like a chain.
And every link was important in its rightful place.

Before me stood my two commitments—one to God and one to my people. They were inextricably bound together. And suddenly, I knew I would rather be on God's side which is stronger than human might.

Then I knew where I should be—not living in comfort, but back in the place where villages and churches were being reunited, where schools and community centers and spirits were being built up, where, amid the terrible noise of violence I could hear the whispers of the Man of Galilee, saying, *Behold, I make all things new.*

Standing, I walked briskly from the room, the old necklace clasped warmly in my hand. I had to find the nearest phone and book a morning flight.

Nazarena and Ghislaine would be surprised to see me.

———————

Elias Chacour continues his work of reconciliation in the strained atmosphere of Israel, hoping to "change hearts, not simply institutions." His ventures are bold, often risky: Palestinian students visit *kibbutzim*; Jewish students live for short periods in Palestinian villages; Jewish and Palestinian educators face each other for head-to-head dialogue. Too, Chacour keeps a grueling schedule lecturing worldwide, always relying on the simple and urgent message of the Beatitudes. And though he is welcomed by friends on all continents, his home address is unchanged:

Fr. Elias Chacour
Ibillin
Galilee
Israel

# References

1. Jonathan Dimbleby, *The Palestinians,* Quartet Books, New York, 1979, p. 86.
2. Jacques de Reynier, *A Jerusalem un Drapeau Flottait sur la Ligne de Feu,* Editions de la Baconniere, Neuchatel, 1950, pp. 71-76. Cited in Walid al Khalidi (Ed.) *From Haven To Conquest,* The Institute of Palestine Studies, Beirut, 1971, pp. 353-356.
3. Dimbleby, p. 35.
4. *Ibid.*
5. Chaim Weizmann, *Trial and Error,* London, 1950, p. 115.
6. Yehoshua Porath, *The Emergence of the Palestine-Arab National Movement 1918-1929,* Frank Cass, London, 1974, pp. 56-57.
7. Walter Laqueur, *A History of Zionism,* Schocken Books, New York, 1976, pp. 215-217.
8. Morris Ernst, *So Far So Good,* Harper & Bros., New York, 1948, pp. 170-177.
9. William A. Eddy, *F.D.R. Meets Ibn Saud,* American Friends of the Middle East, New York, 1954, pp. 36-37.
10. Elmer Berger, *Who Knows Better Must Say So,* The Institute of Palestine Studies, Beirut, p. 64. Cited in David Hirst, *The Gun and the Olive Branch: The Roots of Violence in the Middle East,* Harcourt, Brace, Jovanovich, New York, 1977, pp. 162-163.
11. Reported in the *Sunday Times,* London, June 15, 1969. Cited in Dimbleby, p. 10.

# *For Further Reading*

*The Arab-Israeli Conflict,* Edited by John Norton Moore, Princeton University Press, 1974.

*The Arab-Israeli Dilemma,* by Fred J. Khouri, Syracuse University Press, 1968.

*The Cairo Documents,* by Mohamed Heikal, Doubleday, 1973.

*The Gun and the Olive Branch: The Roots of Violence in the Middle East,* by David Hirst, Harcourt, Brace, Jovanovich, 1977.

*History of Palestine,* by Jacob De Haas, McMillan, 1934.

*A History of Zionism,* by Walter Lacqueur, Shocken Books, 1976.

*The Middle East, Yesterday and Today,* Edited by David W. Miller and Clark D. Moore, Praeger, 1970.

*The Non-Violent Alternative,* by Thomas Merton, Farrar, Straus, Giroux, revised edition 1980.

*The Palestinians,* by Jonathan Dimbleby, Quartet Books, 1979.

*The Politics of Jesus,* by John Howard Yoder, Eerdmans, 1972.

*The Thirteenth Tribe,* by Arthur Koestler, Random House, 1976.

*Whose Promised Land?* by Colin Chapman, Lion Publishing, 1983.